Prophecy today

# PROPHECY TODAY

## A further word from God?

Jim Thompson

EVANGELICAL PRESS

EVANGELICAL PRESS
Faverdale North, Darlington, DL3 0PH, England

e-mail: sales@evangelicalpress.org

Evangelical Press USA
P. O. Box 825, Webster, New York 14580, USA

e-mail: usa.sales@evangelicalpress.org

web: http://www.evangelicalpress.org

First published 2008

**British Library Cataloguing in Publication Data available**

ISBN 13  978 085234 673 0                    ISBN  0 85234 673 5

Printed and bound in Great Britain by Biddles Ltd

# Contents

# Foreword

This book deals with a question that no twenty-first-century Christian can afford to ignore: does God-given prophecy continue in today's church, or doesn't it? And, if it does, can those who announce such prophecies sometimes get things wrong?

Christ's sheep love the voice of the Good Shepherd. If he is speaking through modern prophecy, they want to listen. If he is not, they want nothing to do with it. But if modern prophecy is a mixture of his voice and the voice of others, they want to know how to tell which is which.

Whatever they may believe about prophecy at the moment, Christians know that their final convictions on any subject must be decided by Scripture. It is there that Jim Thompson's important book points us, in a study which is clear, brief, thorough and convincing. The tone of his writing is brotherly and everything is pitched at a level which most readers will find accessible.

Some of us recall that it is now over thirty years since Jim Thompson set himself to examine this subject and the countless issues related to it. He has not gone into print in a hurry! In commending his book, I want to express my hope that it will be read very widely and taken seriously. If this happens, many modern churches may well be saved from disaster.

**Stuart Olyott**

# Acknowledgements

This book makes few claims to originality and my indebtedness to others, past and present, is manifest on almost every page. I am glad to acknowledge my debt to friends who over many years have helped and encouraged me in the preparation of this book.

Particular thanks must go to two people. In the providence of God it was Stuart Olyott who laid the scriptural foundations for my life in my first years as a Christian. For his help and encouragement through the years — and for kindly agreeing to write the foreword — I am deeply grateful.

My special thanks must go to my wife Cilla. Without her encouragement, support and sacrifice, this book would have remained no more than wishful thinking.

Underlying every human support is of course the grace of our glorious God. It is my humble prayer that this book may glorify him and his prophetic Word.

# INTRODUCTION

# Introduction

It is now over one hundred years since the Azusa Street Revival in Los Angeles, California, and with that the beginning of the Pentecostal movement. Some sixty years later we have the beginning of the 'Charismatic Movement' as churches in the mainline denominations started to adopt aspects of Pentecostal theology and practice. Since these beginnings the subject of prophecy has been catapulted high up the agenda for evangelicals. What is the nature of prophecy? How can the true be distinguished from the false? What is the relationship between the prophecy of the Old and New Testaments? And, especially, should we expect that the prophetic gift that was given to the New Testament churches is still to be experienced by the churches of today?

These are questions of great significance for every true Bible-believing Christian. Prophecy is a gift of the Holy Spirit that brings the word of God to his people. It is the deep desire of all believers that they should not grieve or quench the Spirit. They want to know the presence of God among them as they meet together. They want to know God's will for them in every area of their lives. If the gift of prophecy can help them in this, then they will gladly embrace it. If God is giving further revelation to his people, then they want to receive it. I am not speaking here of God's providential guiding of his people through burdens laid on their hearts or through insights of extraordinary wisdom. All Christians (as far as I know) believe that God's presence continues with his people in these ways. By 'prophecy' I mean a further word from God. If God still speaks in this way, then his people must not ignore it.

On the other hand, however, if God *has* withdrawn the gift from his people, if they are now to be led entirely by the written Word found in the Scriptures, then the Lord's people will stand firm against any claimed further revelations. They will remember that watch cry of the Reformation, '*Sola Scriptura*' — 'Scripture alone'. They will remember the examples in church history of prophetic movements that have ended in disaster (such as the Montanists of the second century and the Irvingites of the nineteenth). They will recall that cults such as the Seventh Day Adventists and the Mormons began through the ministry of prophets and prophetesses. And they will give themselves wholeheartedly to the study of their Bibles, remembering that the words of Scripture are 'living and powerful, and sharper than any two-edged sword' (Heb. 4:12).

The subject of the gift of prophecy is one therefore that raises issues that are close to the heart of those who love the Lord. It is also an issue that currently divides evangelicals. Perhaps in the mercy of God he will lead his people into unity of thinking on this matter. Until then it remains the duty of the people of God to seek further light and to continue to embrace those with different views in a spirit of humility and love.

# I.
# THE DISTINGUISHING CHARACTERISTICS OF PROPHECY IN ISRAEL

True and false prophecy
The origins of prophecy in Israel
The messenger formula
Collaboration from the New Testament
Were there different kinds of prophecy in Israel?
Prophecy in the Gospels

# 1.
# The distinguishing characteristics of prophecy in Israel

The importance of prophecy to the spiritual life and health of the nation of Israel can hardly be overstated. Its centrality to godliness is evidenced by the fact that the Old Testament Scriptures are frequently referred to simply as 'the Law and the Prophets' (e.g. Matt. 7:12; 22:40; Acts 24:14) — and, of course, even the law was given through a prophet!

In the following survey it is not at all my aim to examine every aspect of prophecy in Israel. Rather we shall be focusing on the chief characteristics of true prophecy, on those characteristics that distinguish it from the false.

## True and false prophecy

In this respect the incident recorded in 1 Kings 22 is very instructive. Here we have two kings, godly Jehoshaphat of Judah and wicked Ahab of Israel, uniting together with the purpose of recapturing a city that the Syrians had taken. Before they go into battle, Jehoshaphat insists that they seek the word of the Lord on the matter (v. 5). Ahab therefore summons the prophets. There are about four hundred of them altogether, but it is just two who become the focus of attention. Zedekiah the son of Chenaanah encourages the kings to fight; Micaiah the son of Imlah prophesies that the battle will bring disaster. One of these (Micaiah) is a true prophet; the other is false. But what is the feature that distinguishes them?

- It is not that Zedekiah was an idolater. Both spoke in the name of the LORD (vv. 11,19).
- It is not that Zedekiah was one of a large group of prophets whereas Micaiah was alone. There were also a large number of true prophets in Israel at that period (cf. 1 Kings 18:13).
- It is not that Zedekiah and the others were professional prophets in the service of the king whereas Micaiah was independent. That may well have been the case, but it is very likely that the prophet Nathan was a court official of King David, yet he was not compromised.
- It is not that Micaiah is distinguished as the true prophet by the fact that he was thrown into prison (v. 27). False prophets also sometimes suffered, as did the prophets of Baal at the time of Elijah, for example (1 Kings 18:40).
- Nor, finally, was the key difference that Zedekiah's prophecy was not literally fulfilled in every detail. Zedekiah 'had made horns of iron for himself; and he said, "Thus says the LORD: 'With these you shall gore the Syrians until they are destroyed'"' (1 Kings 22:11). No one denounced Zedekiah as a false prophet on the grounds that these horns would not actually be the key weapon in the battle! It was recognized by all that

symbolism was being used, something that was very common among true prophets (see especially Ezekiel).

What then was the distinguishing feature of the true prophet? Simply this: the words of Micaiah proved true. Ahab was killed in the battle. Micaiah had received revelation from the Lord, and he had faithfully passed it on.

## The origins of prophecy in Israel

By the time we come to Micaiah, of course, there have been prophets in Israel for many centuries. The first person named as a prophet is Abraham (Gen. 20:7). The reference speaks of his special relationship with God so that his prayer is effective; other passages record occasions when God spoke to him directly (e.g. Gen. 12:1,7; 15:1, etc.).

The definitive passage on prophecy is found in the context of Moses some four hundred years later. It arises as Moses is warning Israel not to listen to soothsayers and diviners. If they desire to know things that are hidden, then God has appointed another way for them:

> *The LORD your God will raise up for you a Prophet like me from your midst, from your brethren. Him you shall hear, according to all you desired of the LORD your God in Horeb in the day of the assembly, saying, 'Let me not hear again the voice of the LORD my God, nor let me see this great fire any more, lest I die.' And the LORD said to me: 'What they have spoken is good. I will raise up for them a Prophet like you from among their brethren, and will put my words in his mouth, and he shall speak to them all that I command him. And it shall be that whoever will*

*not hear my words, which he speaks in my name, I will require it
of him. But the prophet who presumes to speak a word in my
name, which I have not commanded him to speak, or who speaks
in the name of other gods, that prophet shall die.' And if you say
in your heart, 'How shall we know the word which the LORD has
not spoken?' — when a prophet speaks in the name of the LORD, if
the thing does not happen or come to pass, that is the thing which
the LORD has not spoken; the prophet has spoken it presumptu-
ously; you shall not be afraid of him* (Deut. 18:15-22).

Several key points arise from this passage:

1. The context of this passage (Israel's need for a
source of supernatural revelation) shows that it should
be understood as promising a succession of prophets
to minister to Israel, as, of course, actually happened.
Nevertheless it finds its ultimate fulfilment in the Lord
Jesus himself (cf. Acts 3:22-26).

2. The function of the prophet is to mediate the
word of God. It answers the desire of Israel at Horeb
that God should not speak to them directly. Instead he
would speak to them through a prophet.

3. The authority of the divine word is not dimin-
ished by this arrangement. God would put his words
in the prophet's mouth; the prophet would speak all
that God commanded him; and any who did not listen
to the message would have to answer to God.

4. The test that Israel could use to recognize false
prophecy was by testing the truth of what was spoken.
Anything that was untrue, including even unfulfilled

prediction, marked out a prophet as false. Such a prophet should be put to death.

It should be noticed here that there would be no toleration in this context of a 'mixed prophet' — a prophet who sometimes got things wrong. It would be *God's words* that the prophet would speak — 'my words' (Deut. 18:18,19); and any departures from absolute truth would result in the prophet's being recognized as false and executed.

It is this high view of prophecy that is maintained throughout the Old Testament. When Moses himself is called God promises him, 'I will be with your mouth and teach you what you shall say' (Exod. 4:12). Hundreds of years later, when Jeremiah is commissioned, we read similar words: 'Then the LORD put forth his hand and touched my mouth, and the LORD said to me: "Behold, I have put my words in your mouth"' (Jer. 1:9).

## The messenger formula

Before we move on from Moses completely, we should note that God instructs him to use the messenger formula, 'Thus says the LORD', when he speaks to Pharaoh (Exod. 4:22). As this formula is repeated several hundred times by the prophets, it is necessary for us to spend some time considering its full implications.

The significance of the messenger formula can be clearly seen from its use in secular contexts. It was commonly used by a servant who had been sent by his master to deliver a message. So, for example, when King Balak sends the princes of Moab to deliver a message to Balaam, they introduce their message with the words, 'Thus says Balak the son of Zippor', and then they proceed to speak in the first person as though they were Balak himself (Num. 22:15-17; see also Gen. 32:4-5; 45:9; 2 Kings 19:2-5). Clearly the intention of this device is to put the messenger very much into the background. He disappears behind his master's words. The one who receives the message is not merely hearing the words and opinions of the messenger but is, in effect, being brought face to face with the master who sent him.

In just the same way, the prophets routinely introduce their oracles with the formula, 'Thus says the LORD', and then speak in the first person as though they were God himself, often saying things that only God could say in the first person. For example, Isaiah declares:

*Thus says the LORD:*
*'Heaven is my throne,*
*And earth is my footstool.*
*Where is the house that you will build me?'*

(Isa. 66:1).

If we are to understand the nature of biblical prophecy then the high claim implicit in the messenger formula must be taken seriously. The prophet is emphatically *not* saying, 'This is what I feel God is leading me to say,' or, 'This is what I believe the Lord is saying,' just as the princes of Moab were not merely giving their opinion of what Balak might want to say. On the contrary, in using the messenger formula the prophets clearly intend to bring their hearers face to face with God himself, unambiguously claiming that the words they speak are the very words of God — 'Thus says *the*

LORD'. In other words, an identity is made between what the prophet says and what God says.

A final witness to the divine authority of the prophets is the judgement that falls on those who oppose or reject God's word through them. Pharaoh rejects the command of God through Moses and judgements devastate Egypt. Hananiah opposes the message of Jeremiah and is struck down dead (Jer. 28:10-17). In the days of Nehemiah the Levites reviewed the sorry history of Israel:

> *For many years you [God] had patience with them [his people],*
> *And testified against them by your Spirit in your prophets.*
> *Yet they would not listen;*
> *Therefore you gave them into the hand of the peoples of the lands*
> (Neh. 9:30).

The word of God had come to the prophets; they had delivered it accurately to the people; the people had hardened their hearts against it, and so judgement had fallen as God had called them to account. Many more such examples of judgements could be given, all proving that the message of the prophets was the very word of God.

## Corroboration from the New Testament

This high view of prophecy that is consistently set forth in the Old Testament is wholehearted accepted in the New Testament. Thus events recorded in the Gospels and in the book of Acts are constantly seen as fulfilments of words spoken by the prophets of Israel (see, for example, Matt. 1:22-23; 2:5-6,15,17-18,23; 3:3; 4:13-16; 8:17; 11:10; 12:16-21;

13:13-15; 15:7-9; 21:4-5,16,42; 26:31,54,56; 27:9-10,35; Acts 1:20; 2:16-21; many other examples could be given).

Jesus himself not only accepted, but also actively taught, the divine authority of prophecy. Thus he chastises his disciples: 'O foolish ones, and slow of heart to believe in all that the prophets had spoken!' (Luke 24:25). For Jesus the prophets *must* be fulfilled (Luke 24:44,46). He came not to destroy the Law and the Prophets, but to fulfil them (Matt. 5:17). He explained his actions in cleansing the temple in terms taken from the books of Isaiah and Jeremiah (Matt. 21:13), and his own death as a fulfilment of Zechariah 13:7 (see Matt. 26:31).

Not surprisingly, the apostles and the early church follow the example of Jesus in this. At the Council of Jerusalem when a vital matter of gospel truth is being contested, it is in large part a quotation from the prophet Amos that settles the issue (Acts 15:15-17). When Paul writes his letter to the Roman church, he takes trouble to show that his gospel is in accord with the teaching of the prophets of old (Rom. 1:2,17; 3:21; 9:25-29; 10:11-21; 11:8-10,26-27, etc.). He has no hesitation in introducing a quotation from the prophet Ezekiel with the words, 'As God has said' (2 Cor. 6:16). In similar vein the writer of Hebrews affirms that 'God ... spoke in times past to the fathers by the prophets' (Heb. 1:1).

It is reserved for the apostle Peter to make what is surely the most categorical and comprehensive assertion of the divine authority of the prophets. In 2 Peter 1:21 we read, 'For prophecy never came by the will of man, but holy men of God spoke as they were moved by the Holy Spirit.' This verse has been commonly used in discussions on the inspiration of Scripture, and quite rightly so when it is considered in its context. However, the immediate application of the verse is to the nature of prophecy, whether or not the prophecy became part of the inscripturated Word. Peter's argument is not, 'Prophecy is included in Scripture and therefore prophecy is true' — quite the opposite. He argues, 'Scripture is prophecy, and therefore Scripture is true'!

The meaning of this verse has been well brought out by B. B. Warfield:

> *In this singularly precise and pregnant statement there are several things which require to be carefully observed. There is, first of all, the emphatic denial that prophecy ... owes its origin to human initiative: 'No prophecy ever was brought [came] by the will of man.' Then, there is the equally emphatic assertion that its source lies in God: it was spoken by men, indeed, but the men who spoke it 'spoke from God'. And a remarkable clause is here inserted, and thrown forward in the sentence that stress may fall on it, which tells us how it could be that men, in speaking, should speak not from themselves, but from God: it was 'as borne [moved; Greek pheromenoi] by the Holy Spirit' that they spoke. Speaking thus under the determining influence of the Holy Spirit, the things they spoke were not from themselves but from God... The term here used [pheromenoi] is a very specific one. It is not to be confounded with guiding, or directing, or controlling, or even leading in the full sense of that word. It goes beyond all such terms, in assigning the effect produced specifically to the active agent. What is 'borne' is taken up by the 'bearer', and conveyed by the 'bearer's' power, not its own, to the 'bearer's' goal, not its own. The men who spoke from God are here declared, therefore, to have been taken up by the Holy Spirit and brought by His power to the goal of His choosing. The things which they spoke under*

*this operation of the Spirit were therefore His things, not theirs.
And that is the reason which is assigned why 'the prophetic word'
[v. 19] is so sure. Though spoken through the instrumentality of
men, it is, by virtue of the fact that these men spoke 'as borne by
the Holy Spirit', an immediately Divine word.*[1]

Thus all that we have said so far has been elegantly
summarized by Peter in this one verse. Without any hesitation or reserve, prophecy is *the word of God.*

## Were there different kinds of prophecy in Israel?

In this context it is only possible to give a brief survey of this
matter. Differences among the prophets can be recognized in
the following areas:

### 1. There were differences in the means of revelation

A key passage here is Numbers 12:6-8. Speaking to Moses,
Miriam and Aaron, the Lord says:

*If there is a prophet among you,
I, the LORD, make myself known to him in a vision;
I speak to him in a dream.
Not so with my servant Moses;
He is faithful in all my house.
I speak with him face to face,
Even plainly, and not in dark sayings;
And he sees the form of the LORD.
Why then were you not afraid
To speak against my servant Moses?*

Here there are three means of revelation mentioned — dreams, visions and the 'face to face' revelation that was given to Moses. For most prophets it was the vision that was the usual means by which God communicated his word to them. Thus Isaiah 1:1 reads: 'The *vision* of Isaiah the son of Amoz, which he *saw* ...' (emphasis added; cf. Ezek. 1:1; Amos 1:1; Obad. 1, etc.).

## 2. There were differences in status among the prophets

Again this can be seen from Numbers 12, the passage quoted above. The Lord speaks these words in answer to the complaint made by Miriam and Aaron about the superior status given to Moses: 'Has the LORD indeed spoken only through Moses? Has he not spoken through us also?' (v. 2). Their assertion was right — Miriam was a prophetess (Exod. 15:20) and Aaron had functioned as Moses' spokesman to Pharaoh (Exod. 4:14-16). However, their inference was wrong — the status of Moses was high above their own. God spoke to him plainly, 'face to face', in a way that far exceeded the revelation given to them. Therefore they should have been afraid to speak against him. In fact the dominant figure of Moses towers over the whole of the Old Testament. After his death it was written that 'Since then there has not arisen in Israel a prophet like Moses, whom the LORD knew face to face, in all the signs and wonders which the LORD sent him to do in the land of Egypt ... and by all that mighty power and all the great terror which Moses performed in the sight of all Israel' (Deut. 34:10-12). In the words of E. J. Young, Moses 'is the human founder and the mediator of the Old Covenant. The prophets belonged to this covenant; they built upon the foundation which Moses had laid.'[2]

### 3. There were differences in behaviour among the prophets

The experience of Ezekiel, who not only saw visions but also was himself swept up into them, seems to have been unusual among the prophets. Equally unusual were the 'ecstatic' experiences of Saul (see 1 Sam. 10:5-13; 18:10; 19:20-24) — though whether he actually functioned as a mediator of the word of God and was therefore a prophet in the full sense is not clear.

### 4. There were differences in the ministries given to the prophets

Some worked alone; others ministered in the groups, often referred to as the 'schools of the prophets', that are mentioned occasionally in the Old Testament (e.g. 1 Sam. 10:5,10; 19:20; 2 Kings 2:3,5,7,15). Some, like Moses and Joshua, gave messages for the whole nation; others were sent to an individual with a personal message (e.g. Nathan was sent to David, 2 Sam. 12:1-15). Still others fulfilled the role of judges so that the people could enquire of God by them (remember Samuel answering Saul's question about his lost donkeys!). Most were sent to the Israelites, but Jonah was also sent to Nineveh.

### 5. There are huge differences in the amount of material that has been recorded and preserved from each prophet

Some, such as Moses and Isaiah, have left behind large books of prophecy. Of others, such as the one hundred prophets of the Lord hidden in caves to save them from Jezebel (1 Kings 18:13), we know absolutely nothing concerning the word they proclaimed.

Other differences could be mentioned: the styles of their writing, the response that they received, the background that they came from, their personal family life, and even the clothes that they wore! Enough has been said, however, to show that there was a tremendous variety in the experiences and roles of the prophets of Israel. The writer of Hebrews was not exaggerating when he wrote that 'God ... in various ways spoke in time past to the fathers by the prophets' (Heb. 1:1). Yet, whatever the method used, it was still God who was speaking. When a prophet speaks as a messenger of God — that is, when he prophesies — then his words are the very words of God. Each of them fulfilled the criteria laid down by Moses concerning true prophecy:

1. The prophet received a revelation from God: 'I ... will put my words in his mouth' (Deut. 18:18).

2. The prophet would infallibly declare it: 'Thus says the LORD...'; 'If the thing does not happen or come to pass, that is the thing which the LORD has not spoken' (Deut. 18:22).

3. That the prophet would be tested was not only anticipated (Deut. 18:21), but actually commanded (Deut. 13:1-5). If a prophecy fell short in doctrine ('Let us go after other gods' — Deut. 13:2) or in predictive accuracy, then the prophet was not from God; he should be put to death.

## Prophecy in the Gospels

This section belongs here because in the Gospels is recorded the continuation of the history of Israel. It is only after Pentecost that we can look at the nature of prophecy in the New Testament church.

This section has a particular importance. Although the Gospels cover only a few decades of life in Israel, those decades followed a period of some four hundred years in which the voice of prophecy had largely fallen silent. During that time great political and cultural changes had taken place. Judah had been under the rule of first the Greek and later the Roman empires. Had these profound changes affected Israel's understanding of the nature of prophecy? Some scholars think that this was indeed the case. Hence Aune writes:

> *Not only is it essential that the Israelite-Jewish prophetic and revelatory traditions be considered in order to understand fully the phenomenon of early Christian prophecy, but the Graeco-Roman oracular and prophetic traditions must also be made part of the picture.*[3]

For Grudem too the existence of a lower standard of prophecy in the surrounding world and in Israel itself in the inter-testamental period forms an important part of his belief that prophecy in the early church was significantly different from its Old Testament counterpart. Is there evidence, then, in the Gospels that a change in understanding of prophecy has taken place? Is prophecy in this context no longer 'the word of God', and therefore unerringly true and authoritative? The two following considerations should convince us that no such change has taken place.

## 1. References to prophets

The first consideration is that when in the Gospels reference is made to 'the prophets' it is invariably the Old Testament prophets that are meant. Several examples will make this clear.

- 'O Jerusalem, Jerusalem, the one who kills the prophets ...' (Luke 13:34). It was the Hebrew prophets that the Jews persecuted.
- '... that the blood of all the prophets which was shed from the foundation of the world may be required of this generation, from the blood of Abel to the blood of Zechariah who perished between the altar and the temple' (Luke 11:50-51). Thus these persecuted prophets are 'all the prophets'. No other prophets therefore are truly prophets, dismissing the claims of all Gentile prophets.
- 'Then he said to them, "O foolish ones, and slow of heart to believe in all that the prophets have spoken! Ought not the Christ to have suffered these things and to enter into his glory?" And beginning at Moses and all the Prophets, he expounded to them in all the Scriptures the things concerning himself' (Luke 24:25-27). Clearly for Jesus and his hearers the revelation from 'all the Prophets' is found in 'all the Scriptures'. Greek and Roman prophets are entirely disregarded.

Many more examples could be given showing that, for Jews in first-century Palestine, 'the prophets' meant the Old Testament prophets. Only these are quoted, and they very frequently are. Of inter-testamental or pagan prophets, with their lower standard of prophecy, there is no hint.

## 2. Examples of prophecy

The second consideration is that the actual examples of
prophecy in the Gospels give no indication that a lower
expectation of prophecy is now current. We shall work
chronologically through the examples given to us, some of
which are brief but still helpful.

- In Luke 1:67 we read that 'Zacharias was filled with
the Holy Spirit, and prophesied...' The connection
made between the Holy Spirit and prophecy is a common feature in the Old Testament. His prophecy included predictions about his son John the Baptist that
were accurately fulfilled (Luke 1:76-79).
- Anna is introduced to us by Luke as 'a prophetess'
(Luke 2:36). All that we are told of her is that she recognized the baby Jesus as being good news 'to all those
who looked for redemption in Jerusalem' (Luke 2:38).
- The next prophet introduced to us in the Gospels is
John the Baptist. We have it on the authority of Jesus
himself that John was a prophet (Luke 7:26). We are
told that he received revelation: 'the word of God came
to' him (Luke 3:2). From the accounts of his ministry
recorded for us, it is evident that he spoke with divine
authority. He made predictions which were accurately
fulfilled: 'One mightier than I is coming' (Luke
3:16-17); 'Behold! The Lamb of God who takes away
the sin of the world' (John 1:29).
- Finally, we have in Jesus the great Prophet of God,
the ultimate fulfilment of the prophecy of Moses: 'I
will raise up for them a Prophet ...' (Deut. 18:17; see
also vv. 15-19). He was recognized as 'a Prophet

mighty in deed and word before God and all the people' (Luke 24:19) and by implication he accepted the title himself (Matt. 13:57; Luke 13:33). He taught with full divine authority — 'Thus says the LORD' has been replaced by 'I say to you' (e.g. Matt. 5:20,22,26,28, etc.). He predicts future events (Mark 8:31; 9:31; 10:32; 11:2; 13:2-37; 14:13-16,18,27,30). In the parable of the wicked vinedressers (Matt. 21:33-46) he portrays himself as the climax and the end of the prophetic line to Israel. He not merely brings the word of God, but *is* the Word of God (John 1:1); he not merely brings the truth but *is* the truth (John 14:6).

In all these examples there is no hint that a lower standard of prophecy is now accepted. We have no examples of a prophet sometimes getting things wrong but still being accepted as a true prophet. On the contrary, predictions are made, and they are fulfilled. The word of God is received, and then declared with authority. There are none here who fall short of the standards set down by Moses.

# 2.
# PROPHECY IN THE NEW TESTAMENT CHURCH

Is there New Testament evidence for a lower view of prophecy
   in the churches?
Is there evidence for continuity in the nature of prophecy
   between Old and New Testaments?
Examples of New Testament prophecy examined

# 2.
# Prophecy in the New Testament church

We come now to consider the gift of prophecy as manifested in the first Christian churches. Up to this point, as we have considered prophecy in Israel, we have seen that the definition given by Moses was reflected throughout the centuries of history covered by the Old Testament and on into the period covered by the Gospels. The question that we must seek to answer now is this: does the prophecy that existed in the first-century churches bear the same features as Old Testament prophecy, or has it undergone a significant change? More specifically, is the New Testament gift of prophecy the pure word of God (and therefore infallible), or is it a mixture of revelation from God with the merely human and fallible words of the prophet?

We shall seek to answer these questions in three stages:

1. In the letters of the New Testament, is there evidence that supports a lower view of the prophecy in the churches?

2. In the letters of the New Testament, is there evidence for continuity in the understanding of the nature of prophecy?

3. What do we find when we consider the actual examples of prophecy in the New Testament church?

## Is there New Testament evidence for a lower view of prophecy in the churches?

First, then, in the letters of the New Testament, is there evidence that supports a lower view of the prophecy in the churches? Several arguments are put forward in favour of this view. The first is that the apostle Paul was influenced in his thinking by the pagan culture in the world around him, which held to a broader (and hence lower) view of prophecy. We have already seen, of course, that Paul had the highest view of the authority of the Old Testament prophets — as far as he was concerned, their words were the words of God. But did he have the same view of the prophets in the churches that he ministered to?

### 1. Was Paul influenced by pagan culture?

Some have pointed to Titus 1:12-13 as giving evidence that Paul had adopted a lower view of prophecy. There we read, 'One of them, a prophet of their own, said, "Cretans are always liars, evil beasts, lazy gluttons." This testimony is true.' Paul is quoting from the Cretan poet Epimenides, who 'was reputed to have knowledge of divine things and to be able to predict future events'.[1] Paul calls him a prophet not because he regards him as one, but because that was his reputation among the Cretans. For Paul, of course, Epimenides would have been a false prophet. Since he was not a messenger of the living God, the God of Israel, but of some pagan god or gods, he was by definition an idolater —

someone who sacrifices to demons (1 Cor. 10:20; cf. 8:4-6). However, on this occasion Paul can quote from him and add the comment: 'This testimony is true.' A false prophet can sometimes have a true insight. (It is interesting to note that when in the Bible we do have an example of a mixed prophet — one who speaks both truth and error — it is a pagan false prophet!)

This does raise the whole question of how likely it is that Paul was influenced at all by pagan thinking when he was so opposed to the core of it — its worship of idols. Especially in a matter such as prophecy, which is so closely related to the god that the prophet represents, it would seem incredible to imagine him turning from a scriptural concept of what prophecy is to a different concept taken from the pagan temples. We can therefore safely agree with the conclusion of Aune that 'Undoubtedly Paul's conception of the prophetic role was primarily informed by Old Testament models.'[2]

## 2. Were the prophets tested, or only their prophecies?

A second argument for a lower standard of prophecy in the New Testament churches concerns the nature of the testing that is to be applied to them. For example, Grudem argues from 1 Thessalonians 5:20-21 that 'It is the prophecies (vs. 20) that are evaluated or judged, not the prophets.'[3] The full passage reads: 'Do not quench the Spirit. Do not despise prophecies. Test all things; hold fast what is good. Abstain from every form of evil' (1 Thess. 5:19-22). From this Grudem deduces that New Testament prophecy must contain a mixture of truth and error, and that it is the purpose of the testing to sort the good from the bad. There are at least three problems with this conclusion, however.

1. It fails to recognize that testing prophets could well involve testing the prophecies that they make. A false prophet can be detected by errors that he makes in his prophecies. It is not therefore a stark choice between testing the prophet and testing the prophecies.

2. It restricts the command to test all things to the prophecies mentioned in the preceding sentence. But in fact it is likely that Paul's intended application is wider. There are many ways of quenching the Spirit. Paul is urging his readers to abstain from every form of evil, not just erroneous prophecy. As Leon Morris writes, 'The words he uses are quite general, and they must be held to apply to all kinds of things, and not simply to claimants to spiritual gifts.'[4]

3. In the Old Testament the purpose of the testing was to distinguish the true prophet from the false. The same is the case in Matthew 7:15-20, where we are told, 'Beware of false prophets ...', and in 1 John 4:1-6, where we read, 'Test the spirits ... because many false prophets have gone out into the world.' Unless we have very good reason to the contrary, we should assume that the same is the case here.

Another passage on testing prophecy that is used by Grudem as evidence of 'mixed prophecy' is 1 Corinthians 14:29: 'Let two or three prophets speak, and let the others judge.' He gives two arguments for his case that fallible prophecy must be spoken of here:

*The context*

The first argument is based on the context in which this command was given. Grudem writes:

*The other passages [he has in mind Matt. 7:15, 1 John 4:1-6 and texts from the Didache] give warnings of strangers coming to the church from outside ... and provide criteria by which they could be tested. But in 1 Cor. 14, Paul is talking about a meeting of those who are already accepted in the fellowship of the church... Rather, the picture is one of several prophets who are known and accepted by the congregation, each speaking in turn. In such a case, it would be very unlikely that they would be 'judged' and declared 'true' prophets again and again, every time they spoke, month after month.*[5]

However, this reconstruction fails to take account of the specific problems in the church at Corinth. From what we can glean from 1 Corinthians, their meetings seem to have been disorderly (cf. 1 Cor. 14:40). There was shameful chaos at the Lord's Supper, including drunkenness (1 Cor. 11:20-21). Speaking in tongues was not being interpreted so that others could understand (1 Cor. 14:6-19). Several prophets were speaking at once (1 Cor. 14:29-31). Under these conditions and with this attitude, it is unlikely that any serious testing of prophets could or would take place. In fact Paul has to teach them the most basic of tests for true prophecy: 'I make known to you that no one speaking by the Spirit of God calls Jesus accursed, and no one can say that Jesus is Lord except by the Holy Spirit' (1 Cor. 12:3).

It would not have been the case, then, that there were 'several prophets who [were] known and accepted by the congregation'. It is to get the church to that stage that Paul gives the instructions concerning testing. When a prophet, following such testing, had become 'known and accepted' (like Agabus, for example) his proclamations could be immediately accepted as the word of God. Even the predictions made by such men could be immediately acted upon, though there was no way that their words could be 'tested' other than by waiting for the fulfilment (cf. Acts 11:27-30).

*The meaning of the Greek word used*

Grudem's second argument for fallible prophecy from 1 Corinthians 14:29 is based on the Greek word that is used for 'judge' (from the verb *diakrinō*). In his *Systematic Theology* he writes:

> When Paul says, 'Let two or three prophets speak, and let the others weigh what is said' (1 Cor. 14:29) [a quite different translation, note, from the NKJV's 'Let the others judge'] he suggests that they should listen carefully and sift the good from the bad, accepting some and rejecting the rest (for this is the implication of the Greek word *diakrinō*, here translated, 'weigh what is said'). We cannot imagine that an Old Testament prophet like Isaiah would have said, 'Listen to what I say and weigh what is said — sort the good from the bad, what you should accept from what you should not accept'! If prophecy had absolute divine authority, it would be sin to do this. But here Paul commands that it be done, suggesting that New Testament prophecy did not have the authority of God's very words.[6]

Grudem is here putting great store on the meaning of one Greek word. Whether it is safe to do so is doubtful. He himself wrote a few years earlier that 'The word [*diakrinō*] has quite a wide range of meanings,' and that 'Since this is not the only possible meaning for *diakrinō*, one cannot say on lexical grounds alone that it absolutely requires this sense in

1 Cor. 14:29.'⁷ In fact another Greek scholar categorically
disagrees with Grudem's interpretation: 'The reference is not
so much to what the prophets say as to the spirits of the
prophets, 12:10.'⁸ And, indeed, it may be better to link
1 Corinthians 14:29 with 1 Corinthians 12:10, where the
subject is again prophecy (along with other gifts) and the
same verb, *diakrinō* (or its cognate noun in some manu-
scripts), is used. There we have part of Paul's listing of the
spiritual gifts: '... to another the working of miracles, to
another prophecy, to another discerning [*diakrinō*] of spirits,
to another different kinds of tongues, to another the interpretation of tongues.' Since the 'discerning of spirits' immediately follows the reference to prophecy, it is natural to
connect the two. The 'discerning' here, then, 'was necessary
... to know whether the inspired speaker ... was actuated by
the Spirit of God, or by some demonic agency (cf. 12:3).'⁹ If
this is the case, then Grudem's argument here is mistaken.
The judging is to determine whether the prophet is true or
false, not to sift good prophecies from bad.

### 3. Did the New Testament prophets have less authority?

A third argument for a lower view of prophecy in the New
Testament church is that the prophets of the first churches
had less authority than their Old Testament counterparts.
Now it is undoubtedly true that the role of the New Testament prophets was restricted in comparison with that of
Moses and Isaiah, for example. It is the apostles who were
the primary agents of revelation after Pentecost. It is they
whom Jesus personally called and trained that they might be
sent out to preach the gospel. It was they who received
special promises of help for this task: 'The Spirit of truth ...
will guide you into all truth' (John 16:13; cf. 14:26). It was the

apostles who uniquely bore witness to the resurrection of Christ.

Since the apostles were the primary agents of revelation, they are put above prophets in Paul's deliberately ordered list: 'God has appointed these in the church: first apostles, second prophets ...' (1 Cor. 12:28). A little later in the same letter he asserts his authority over all in the church who are spiritually gifted, including prophets: 'If anyone thinks himself to be a prophet or spiritual, let him acknowledge that the things which I write to you are the commandments of the Lord' (1 Cor. 14:37).

Does the undeniable fact that the apostles had a higher status than the New Testament prophets mean, then, that these prophets were fallible in their declarations, that they were 'mixed prophets' who sometimes got it right but also sometimes got it wrong? No, it does not mean that at all. A parallel can be drawn here with prophecy in the Old Testament. We have already seen that the Old Testament prophets did not all enjoy equality of status. On the contrary, the authority of Moses towers over that of the prophets who succeeded him, except for John the Baptist (Matt. 11:11). It was the word of the Lord given through Moses that instituted the prophetic office and laid down the tests by which every later claimant to the gift of prophecy would be judged.

Isaiah then, mighty prophet though he was, still came under the authority of Moses. If Isaiah had proclaimed oracles that contradicted the revelation given through Moses, then it would have been Isaiah who would have been rejected as a false prophet. The later prophets built on the foundation that Moses had laid, but if they spoke contrary to that foundation, then God had not sent them. Thus Jeremiah recognized that other prophets of his day were false because they were wicked themselves, they confirmed the nation in its wickedness by preaching 'peace' and they prophesied by Baal (Jer. 23:9-22) — in other words, when they were measured against the touchstone of those things revealed through Moses they were found wanting.

Of course a true prophet would never speak contrary to Moses because it is the same God who speaks through them both. Since both speak the very words of God, there could never be any contradiction. It is the same with the apostles and the New Testament prophets. Because both were inspired by the one Spirit they would never contradict one another. But if conflicting messages were ever given, then it would be the prophet who would be recognized as being false. It is this status that Paul is asserting for himself in 1 Corinthians 14:37. He, along with the other apostles, is laying the foundation by which all other revelations are to be tested. Any who do not acknowledge this authority are not to be recognized (cf. Gal. 1:8-9).

Although the fact that they were subject to the apostles does not imply that the Christian prophets were fallible, it did have implications for their role. It was *the apostles* who had witnessed the fulness of revelation that was manifested in Christ (John 1:1,14) and it was *their* commission now to declare 'the whole counsel of God' (Acts 20:27). It was within this limiting framework that the New Testament prophets ministered. It was, very definitely, 'First apostles, second prophets'.

To conclude, we have considered arguments put forward for the case that New Testament prophecy was of a lower level (mixed with error) than Old Testament prophecy, and we have found those arguments wanting. Now we move on to the second stage of our enquiry: we shall now search the letters of the New Testament for evidence that Christian prophecy was in fact in continuity with its Old Testament counterpart.

## Is there evidence for continuity in the nature of prophecy between Old and New Testaments?

Secondly, then, in the letters of the New Testament, is there evidence for continuity in the understanding of the nature of prophecy?

### 1. The foundational nature of the Old Testament

We begin with a few general considerations. The Old Testament was the Bible of the early church, accepted without reserve by Jesus and the apostles as Holy Scripture. As such it had a completely different status among the first Christians from that accorded to any other writings. The works of Greek philosophers, Latin poets and other Jewish writings may have been interesting and even edifying reading, but the Old Testament was the very Word of God. It had an all-pervasive influence upon the authors of the New Testament — they are constantly quoting from it and alluding to it. More significantly, they build their own beliefs upon it, reading it as Christian Scripture, the foundation of their own faith. Much that might otherwise have had to have been worked out from scratch therefore receives relatively slight attention in the New Testament, not because it is unimportant, but because it can be assumed as already established from the Old Testament.

Given this pervasive influence of the Old Testament upon the New Testament authors, and their unquestioning acceptance of it, the presumption has to be that it is upon the Old Testament doctrine of prophecy that they are drawing when they designate certain people in the church as 'prophets'. We have already seen that it is unlikely that Jewish writers would be significantly influenced by Gentile conceptions of prophecy. It is the Old Testament concept that must be our starting point in understanding Christian prophecy.

## 2. The linguistic evidence

The normal Greek word for a New Testament prophet is *prophētēs*. It and its cognate forms are used of Agabus and the other prophets from Syria, of Judas and Silas, of the spiritual gift of prophecy, and of the prophets who ministered at Corinth and other New Testament churches (Acts 11:27-28; 13:1; 15:32; 19:6; 1 Cor. 12:10; 14:29; Eph. 4:11; 1 Thess. 5:20; etc.). It is significant that when the Old Testament was translated into Greek (the Septuagint) the normal Hebrew word for a prophet (*nābhî*, occurring several hundred times) was invariably translated by *prophētēs*. The Septuagint was widely read not only by Jews, but also by Christians — for many of them it was their Old Testament, and many of the New Testament quotations of the Old are taken from it. Thus, even before the New Testament was written, there was already a consistent usage of *prophētēs* for the Old Testament prophet. The New Testament authors followed this practice in their own writings — Isaiah, Samuel, David, Jeremiah, Daniel, Joel, Jonah, Elisha, Hosea, Amos, Micah, Habakkuk and Zechariah are all referred to in the New Testament using the word *prophētēs*, as well as there being numerous references to prophets in general. It is particularly striking that in

the *same letter* Paul uses *prophētēs* and its cognates for the Old
Testament prophets and for the spiritual gift of prophecy
(Rom. 1:2; 3:21; 12:6).

The linguistic evidence, then, strongly implies an essential
similarity between the prophets of the Old and the New
Testaments. The Septuagint had already established *prophētēs*
as the proper Greek word for an Old Testament prophet, and
the New Testament authors endorsed this by using *prophētēs*
for the same purpose themselves. It is very significant,
therefore, that they should also use this same term for the
New Testament prophets — something that would be very
strange if the New Testament prophets were of an essentially
different nature from those of the Old Testament. It would,
of course, be going too far to deduce that there were no
differences at all between the two, but on the other hand it
would be very odd to give them the same title if there were
fundamental differences between them. This title was chosen
for them by the New Testament authors, and the fact that
they were happy to use it for the Old Testament and New
Testament prophets alike strongly suggests that the two
were essentially the same.

## 3. Prophets receive revelation

We can go further than this, however, in looking for evidence of continuity between prophecy of the Old and the
New Testaments. The key features of Old Testament prophecy that we noted in an earlier chapter are also seen in the
New Testament prophets. Just as 'the word of the LORD'
came to the Old Testament prophets, so the New Testament
prophets received revelation (1 Cor. 14:30; Eph. 3:5; Acts
11:28; 21:10-11; also the whole book of Revelation!). Hence
when Paul draws up his lists of spiritual gifts he always

distinguishes between prophets and teachers — both proclaim the word, but the prophet receives the message by revelation rather than by study (Rom. 12:6-7; 1 Cor. 12:28-29; Eph. 4:11).

## 4. Prophets predict future events

Another key feature of Old Testament prophets was that they commonly predicted future events. This was of course by no means the whole of their ministry, but the definitive passage on prophets leads us to expect that it would be an integral part of it (Deut. 18:21-22) — which indeed it was throughout the Old Testament. This same feature also occurs regularly among the New Testament prophets. Agabus predicts a worldwide famine and the arrest of the apostle Paul (Acts 11:28; 21:10-11), and the book of Revelation contains many predictions.

## 5. Prophets are to be tested

A third key feature of Old Testament prophets was the requirement that they be tested (Deut. 13:1-5; 18:21-22). We have already seen that to test the prophets was a duty laid upon the New Testament church, commanded by the Lord and by the apostle John as well as by Paul (Matt. 7:15-20; 1 John 4:1-6; 1 Cor. 14:29; 1 Thess. 5:20-21).

To summarize then, the pervasive influence of the Old Testament on the authors of the New Testament, the fact that *prophētēs* is routinely used by the New Testament authors for both Old Testament and New Testament prophets and the recognition that key features of Old Testament prophecy are also associated with the New Testament gift all

point us to the same conclusion — that in all essentials Old
Testament and New Testament prophecy are the same. In
particular, this would mean that a difference as profound as
that proposed by Grudem — that the Old Testament prophets spoke the very words of God but the New Testament
prophets were 'mixed', sometimes proclaiming truth but also
sometimes error — is completely unthinkable.

But will this conclusion be confirmed when we examine
in detail the actual examples that we are given of prophecy
in the New Testament church? It is to that question that we
must now turn our attention.

## Examples of New Testament prophecy examined

Thirdly, what do we find when we consider the actual
examples of prophecy in the New Testament church?

There are in fact very few examples of prophecy in the
New Testament church recorded for us. Luke records just
two undisputed examples for us in the Acts of the Apostles,
both of them involving the prophet Agabus (Acts 11:27-30;
21:10-14); two other examples from Acts may probably be
added to these (Acts 13:2; 21:4). The fullest and clearest
example is the book of Revelation itself.

### 1. The book of Revelation

If we may begin with the book of Revelation, let us first note
that this book clearly is a prophecy. Right at the beginning
we read, 'Blessed is he who reads and those who hear the
words of this *prophecy*' (Rev. 1:3, emphasis added). Near the
end we read; 'Blessed is he who keeps the words of the
*prophecy* of this book' (Rev. 22:7, emphasis added). It is a

prophecy and is to be accepted on that basis. What does that mean? It means that it is to be received as the very word of God. Hence we have the emphatic warning in the last chapter: 'For I testify to everyone who hears the words of the prophecy of this book: If anyone adds to these things, God will add to him the plagues that are written in this book; and if anyone takes away from the words of the book of this prophecy, God shall take away his part from the Book of Life, from the holy city, and from the things which are written in this book' (Rev. 22:18-19). The idea that prophecy in the New Testament church was fallible finds no basis here.

## 2. The prophecies of Agabus

Let us turn now to the book of Acts and to the prophet Agabus. Is there evidence here of fallible prophecy? Not in Acts 11:27-30, where Luke records his prophecy of an approaching famine. The following data is relevant:

    1. Luke describes Agabus as a prophet (*prophētēs*, Acts 11:27-28), precisely the same title that he uses of Elisha, Joel, David, Samuel, Amos, Isaiah and Habakkuk (Luke 4:27; Acts 2:16,30; 3:24; 7:42,48-49; 8:28; 13:40-41). This would be misleading, to say the least, if there was a fundamental difference between the Old Testament and the New Testament office.

    2. Luke tells us that Agabus spoke 'by the Spirit' (Acts 11:28), a phrase that echoes expressions often used of the Old Testament prophets (see, for example, 2 Sam. 23.2; 2 Chr. 15:1; 20:14-15; 24:20; Ezek. 3:24).

    3. The prediction was fulfilled: '... which also happened in the days of Claudius Caesar' (Acts 11:28).

4. On the authority of his prediction, the disciples all gave towards the relief of those who would be affected by this approaching famine. In other words, they believed without doubt that Agabus' message was the word of God.

All that is recorded here is completely in harmony with Old Testament prophecy: a revelation is given to the prophet; he communicates it by the Spirit; the godly accept it and obey; and the predictive element is fulfilled.

If the fallible prophecy viewpoint has no support from the first prophecy of Agabus, is it supported by his second prophecy in Acts 21:10-14? On the contrary, the link here with Old Testament prophecy is even stronger!

1. Note that Agabus prefaces his message with the solemn words, 'Thus says the Holy Spirit' (Acts 21:11), an unmistakeable echo of the 'Thus says the LORD' of the prophets of old. Lenski comments on this: 'Agabus quotes the very words of the Spirit exactly as the ancient prophets did. If this is not Verbal Inspiration, pray, what is?'[10]

2. He employs a symbolical action such as was commonly used by Old Testament prophets: 'He took Paul's belt, bound his own hands and feet, and said...' (Acts 21:11).

3. We note once again that his words were received as being undoubtedly true. Luke records the response of the hearers: 'Now when we heard these things, both we and those from that place pleaded with him not to go up to Jerusalem' (Acts 21:12), and verse 13 adds that they pleaded with tears. Without

hesitation the prophet's message was accepted as being from the Lord himself.

At this point we must pause and ask the question: 'Was Agabus' prophecy actually fulfilled?' It has been argued, particularly by Grudem, that in fact it was erroneous at two points. Grudem writes, 'Using OT standards, Agabus would have been condemned as a false prophet, because in Acts 21:27-35 neither of his predictions are fulfilled.'[11] We shall examine each of these alleged errors in turn.

*The Jews would bind Paul*

Firstly, Agabus predicted that *the Jews* would bind (Greek *deō*) Paul, but in fact Luke records twice that it was the Romans who bound him (Acts 21:33; 22:29 — the Greek word *deō* is used both times). Was Agabus therefore in error? Hardly — unless, that is, we insist that prophecy must be interpreted in a strictly literal manner. The Jews did 'bind' Paul, though they did so in a metaphorical sense: they 'seized Paul, and dragged him out of the temple' (Acts 21:30). That *deō* can carry this metaphorical sense of 'confined' or 'constrained' is confirmed by many New Testament examples. In fact in the preceding chapter we read of Paul telling the Ephesian elders, 'I go bound [*deō*] in the Spirit to Jerusalem' (Acts 20:22) — a clear example of metaphorical use. So Agabus predicts that the Jews at Jerusalem will bind Paul, and that is what they do, though metaphorically. That the Romans also bind Paul may be irrelevant to the prophecy.

Perhaps to some this will seem to be too easy a solution. However, it must not be forgotten that such metaphorical language is a very common feature in biblical prophecy. To give just a few examples: 'Zion shall be ploughed like a field' (Micah 3:12); 'Prepare the way of the Lord; make straight in the desert a highway for our God' (Isa. 40:3-4); 'The people who walked in darkness have seen a great light' (Isa. 9:2); 'I will establish one shepherd over them, and he shall feed them — my servant David' (Ezek. 34:23). Scores of similar examples could be given.[12]

In particular, the symbolical actions used by many prophets were a kind of 'wordless metaphor'. For example, when Jeremiah put bonds and yokes on his neck (Jer. 27:2), it was a non-literal sign of the bondage that would come upon nations that refused the word of God. When we read that Zedekiah the son of Chenaanah made himself horns of iron and told Ahab and Jehoshaphat, 'Thus says the LORD: "With these you shall gore the Syrians until they are destroyed"' (1 Kings 22:11), we do not reject him as a false prophet because horns of iron were not used in the battle! That is understood by all as a symbol. He is rejected as false because the two kings were defeated — in other words, the point of the prophecy, which the symbolical action and metaphorical language helped to convey, was not fulfilled. With Agabus the reverse is the case: the point of his prophecy is fulfilled — Paul was seized by the Jews.

### The Jews would deliver Paul into the hands of the Gentiles

The second alleged error in Agabus' prophecy is that in fact the Jews did not deliver Paul into the hand of the Gentiles. Grudem argues that the Greek word *paradidōmi* ('to deliver', 'hand over') implies that the act is done 'actively, consciously, willingly'.[13] Since the Jews did not do this — on the contrary, it is clear from Acts that they wanted to kill Paul themselves — he claims that Agabus' prediction appears to be erroneous.

Grudem's interpretation of this Greek word is open to question, however.

First, the standard lexicons that I have checked do not explicitly support his claim that *paradidōmi* implies that the act is done 'actively, consciously, willingly'.

Secondly, there are examples of the use of the word in the New Testament that do not appear to fit his tightly drawn definition. One example occurs in Luke 23:25. There we read that Pilate 'delivered [*paradidōmi*] Jesus to their will'. The context makes it clear that, far from Pilate willingly handing Jesus over, he did it under constraint; it was not his but 'their will' (i.e. that of the Jews) that was fulfilled. An even more pertinent example occurs in Acts 28:17. There we have the words of Paul: 'I was delivered [*paradidōmi*] as a prisoner from Jerusalem into the hands of the Romans.' Delivered by whom? Since it was 'into the hands of the Romans', it must have been by the Jews. But when we read Luke's account starting from Paul's arrest in Acts 21 through to Acts 28 we do not find any occasion when the Jews actively, consciously, willingly, handed Paul over. Contrary to the view of Grudem, that does not seem to be an essential aspect of the meaning of *paradidōmi*.

*The fulfilment of Agabus' prophecy*

What we do in fact find in these chapters is the accurate fulfilment of Agabus' words. When the Jews seize Paul, the Romans have to intervene. They do so simply to quell the uproar — they have no charges against Paul themselves. However, the Jerusalem Jews persist in seeking Paul's life until finally he has to appeal to Caesar for a trial (Acts 25:11).

This was not what the Romans had wanted; on the contrary, it put Felix in the embarrassing position of having to send a prisoner before Caesar with no specific charges made against him! (Acts 25:26-27). At this point Agabus' prophecy is completely fulfilled: Paul is in 'the hands [i.e. the power] of the Gentiles', having to answer to Roman (not Jewish) law, and he was delivered into their hands by the deliberate policy of the Jerusalem Jews in sustaining their prosecution of Paul.

That, at least, seems to be how Paul himself viewed the course of events in Acts 21 – 25. When he arrives in Rome and has the opportunity to speak to the leaders of the Jewish community there, he tells them (in the words we have already quoted) that he 'was delivered as a prisoner from Jerusalem into the hands of the Romans' (Acts 28:17). Agabus predicted that 'the Jews at Jerusalem ... [will] deliver him into the hands of the Gentiles', and Paul years later records that he 'was delivered [by the Jews] as a prisoner from Jerusalem into the hands of the Romans'. Thus, at least as far as Paul was concerned, Agabus' prophecy was accurately fulfilled.

### 3. The setting apart of Barnabas and Paul

The two remaining examples in Acts can be considered much more briefly.

In Acts 13:1 we are told that in the church at Antioch 'There were certain prophets and teachers.' In the next verse we read: 'As they ministered to the Lord and fasted, the Holy Spirit said, "Now separate to me Barnabas and Saul for the work to which I have called them."' Now it is possible that the Holy Spirit spoke directly to those gathered, as he did earlier to Peter (Acts 10:19). However, the alternative view — that the Holy Spirit spoke by one of the prophets present — would seem to be more likely. That, after all, was the precise function of the prophet.

Furthermore, when we read of Paul telling the Ephesian elders that 'the Holy Spirit testifies in every city' of the troubles awaiting him (Acts 20:23), and when we recall that the only actual examples of this that are recorded for us refer to human agency being used (Acts 21:4,11), this would add further support to the view that a prophet was also employed in Acts 13:2.

If that is the case then Acts 13:2 provides a further example of infallible prophetic revelation. The message is prefaced by the words, 'The Holy Spirit said'. As with the prophets of old, it is given in the first person: 'Now separate to *me* ... *I* have called them' (emphasis added). And it was accepted without reservation — Barnabas and Paul were sent out.

## 4. The warning given to Paul by the disciples at Tyre

The last of our possible examples is in Acts 21:4: 'And finding disciples, we stayed there seven days. They told Paul through the Spirit not to go up to Jerusalem.' These disciples at Tyre gave Paul a message concerning the future, doing so 'through the Spirit', and so it is natural to conclude that they had the gift of prophecy.

The obvious question arises: 'Why did Paul disobey this message?' Three proposed solutions will be considered:

1. Paul believed that New Testament prophecy was fallible and could be disregarded without blame. But this solution clashes with the view of prophecy given in the other, fuller examples discussed above. It

is also difficult to reconcile with the text itself; these
disciples spoke 'through the Spirit', not 'in the flesh',
as would surely have been the case for a mistaken
prophecy.

2.  Paul was in fact disobedient to the Holy Spirit —
that is, he sinned. But again this solution immediately
faces problems. We have already been told twice in the
preceding chapters that it was the Spirit who was leading him to Jerusalem! (Acts 19:21; 20:22).

3.  What happens at Tyre is the same as what occurs
a little later at Caesarea (Acts 21:11-14). It is revealed to
the disciples 'through the Spirit' that there is trouble
ahead for Paul, so they add their own (erroneous) interpretation, which is that Paul should not go. As F. F.
Bruce comments on this verse, 'The inspired vision
foresaw the difficulties and dangers that lay ahead of
Paul (cf. v. 11); they drew the conclusion that he
should not go up to Jerusalem (cf. v. 12).'[14] On this understanding of the text the problems arise only because
of the brevity of Luke's account. This interpretation
then has the advantage of being in line with the preceding and following contexts, and with the understanding of prophecy in the rest of Acts. This is the
view of Calvin, John Stott, I. Howard Marshall and
other commentators.[15]

Our conclusion from the book of Acts, then, is that New
Testament prophecy is of the same essential nature as that of
the Old Testament. In particular:

• Agabus is called a prophet just as Moses and other
  Old Testament prophets are.

- He uses the messenger formula ('Thus says the Holy Spirit') and symbolic actions.
- His predictions are always fulfilled.
- On each occasion that a prophecy is given the church responds with full confidence in the truth of the prophecy. This is so whether the revelation gave personal guidance to individuals (as with Barnabas and Paul), or general guidance to a fellowship (Agabus' prophecy of the famine). Both commands and predictions were fully accepted, even when large amounts of money or great commitment from individuals were involved, and even when these messages could not be 'proved' from Scripture.

In other words, in Acts as well as in the book of Revelation, prophecy as it existed in the New Testament church resembled its Old Testament counterpart in that it too was the infallible word of God. And if that is the case, the fallible prophecy of today's churches is in need of serious reconsideration. It is to this matter that we must now turn our attention.

# 3.
# PROPHECY NOW

# 3

# PROPHECY Now

# 3.
# Prophecy now

We have now completed our study of the nature of the gift of prophecy. This led to the conclusion that we have a consistent picture given throughout Scripture: both the Old and New Testaments portray prophecy as God himself speaking through human agency, so that the word given is an entirely divine word. In other words, prophecy is inerrant. Nowhere in Scripture is it a mixture of the words of man with those of God and therefore subject to error. On the contrary, the whole biblical understanding of the nature of prophecy is summarized in the words of the apostle Peter: 'Prophecy never came by the will of man, but holy men of God spoke as they were moved by the Holy Spirit' (2 Peter 1:21). Our task now is to see how modern-day prophecy compares with this standard.

## The character of prophecy now

It is immediately apparent that Pentecostal and Charismatic prophecy is in a different world from that of the infallible biblical prophecy described above. Take, for example, the following quotations from Pentecostal and Charismatic writers:

*[Prophecy has] varying degrees of genuine inspiration ... the ordinary inspiration of prophetic utterance (not infallible) ... can possibly cover a tremendously wide range of degrees of purity and power.*[1]

*A man may be strongly used in the prophetic office, and yet may be completely wrong from time to time... We should also be careful of personal, directive prophecy ... and extreme caution should be used in receiving any alleged directive or predictive prophecy.*[2]

*Uncritical acceptance must not be given to the prophet's words... For although the prophet is the instrument of the Spirit of God he is not infallible, for he is still human and he may err. The discerning congregation must therefore be ready to correct him.*[3]

*The content of many modern prophecies is a mixture of divine and human origin.*[4]

In his *Systematic Theology* (1994) Wayne Grudem writes:

*So prophecies in the church today should be considered merely human words, not God's words, and are not equal to God's words in authority ... there is almost uniform testimony from all sections of the Charismatic movement that prophecy is imperfect and impure, and will contain elements that are not to be obeyed or trusted. For example, Bruce Yocum, the author of a widely used book on prophecy, writes, 'Prophecy can be impure — our own thoughts or ideas can get mixed into the message we receive.'*[5]

In the same chapter Grudem also quotes with approval the words of Michael Harper: 'Prophecies which tell other people what they are to do — are to be regarded with great suspicion.'[6]

The list of quotations expressing this belief that modern prophets are fallible could be extended almost indefinitely. But the implication to be drawn from the biblical teaching on prophecy is that all the people that these authors have in mind are false prophets! According to the Scriptures, a 'prophet' who prophesies error is a false prophet — under the old covenant he would have been put to death. This modern 'prophecy' is fundamentally different from biblical prophecy. The early Christians did not treat Agabus' famine prophecy with 'extreme caution'; on the contrary, they immediately determined to send relief! (Acts 11:29). For these Christians 'uncritical acceptance' *must be given* to the prophet's words! Agabus had been recognized as a true prophet of the Lord (Acts 11:27-28), and therefore his declarations were received as the very word of God.

In fact churches today have very good reason for being cautious about accepting the messages of their 'prophets'. There have been many instances of messages that have been completely wrong. A few examples will be sufficient to illustrate the point.

In 1974 David Wilkerson (of *The Cross and the Switchblade* fame) published a book entitled *The Vision*. It was 'a vision of five tragic calamities coming upon the earth' and claimed to be 'an urgent message from God's throne room'. It contains the prediction that 'More than one-third of the United States will be designated a disaster area within the next few years.' This is a very specific prophecy that has clearly not been fulfilled.[7]

Our next example is given by Jack Deere, taken from a message given by him in 1994. Jack Deere was one of the Kansas City Prophets and had connections with the Vineyard Movement, and in particular with the Toronto Airport Vineyard, home of the 'Toronto Blessing'. In warning people not to shy away from prophecy because of its messy nature, Deere describes how a 'wonderfully effective prophetic minister' came before a group of 800 high school young people. He began to give prophetic words about youth in the audience. Then he called up a young eighteen-year-old man and said to him, ' "You're into pornography. And the Lord says you have to repent." The young man begins to cry. Sits back down. The only problem was, the young man wasn't into pornography. He was publicly humiliated before 800 high school kids. We had to go back to his church, apologize to his whole church, apologize to the whole conference. It was a horrible mess.'[8]

In 1990 Paul Cain, an American preacher associated with the Kansas City Prophets, prophesied that there would be a great spiritual revival in Europe. This, he predicted, would begin in London in October 1990 and spread throughout the British Isles and across into the continent of Europe. The prophecy was confirmed and repeated by other well-known 'prophets' of the time. It was therefore widely accepted by Charismatics and evangelicals in Britain, and special meetings were held. To the great disappointment of many, no revival occurred.

Since it is widely admitted by Charismatics that prophecy today is fallible, it is unnecessary to give more examples. Anyone who has been to meetings where specific predictive prophecies have been given (perhaps most commonly about healings) will be able to add their own examples of failed

prophecies to this list. This is not to deny that some prophecies have been fulfilled — a spokesman for the Vineyard
Movement estimated that 'The general level of prophetic
revelation in the church was about 65% accurate.'[9] However,
even some psychics would claim a better record than this
and it falls far below the biblical standard of 100% accuracy
for true prophecy.

It is hard to avoid the conclusion that prophecy today is
not a revival of the New Testament gift. The gulf between
the two is unbridgeable. One is the very word of God; the
other is the all-too-fallible word of men.

This gulf between the prophecy of the New Testament
church and that claimed today raises another question:
'Does the New Testament give any indication that the gift
of prophecy was not to continue beyond the time of the
apostles?' It is to that question that we must now turn our
attention.

## A cessation of prophecy?

As we shall see later in the chapter, the vast majority of
evangelicals living before the beginning of the Charismatic
Movement in the 1960s believed that the gift of prophecy
was no longer given by God after the days of the apostles.

It was not simply that the question of prophecy did not
arise — a number of groups did claim that they had prophets among them. The Mormons base their teaching on the
revelations given to Joseph Smith, the first of which is said
to have been received in 1820. The teachings concerning
Sabbath-keeping and the investigative judgement that are
specific to the Seventh-Day Adventists are based on visions

purportedly given to Hiram Edson and Ellen G. White from 1844 onwards. The openness to new revelations in the Roman Catholic Church continued, as is illustrated by the canonization in 1933 of Bernadette Soubirous of Lourdes. In 1858 she had claimed to have seen visions of the Virgin Mary, who introduced herself as 'the Immaculate Conception' — a doctrine that is now official Roman Catholic teaching.

Other examples of 'prophets', 'visions' and 'revelations' could be given, but these are sufficient to make the point that evangelicals did not omit prophecy from their church life simply because the subject had been forgotten. Prophecy has always been a live issue! Why, then, did evangelicals from the Reformation until the 1960s not seek the gift? Because they believed that the Scriptures themselves taught that revelation had ceased and that consequently the gift had been discontinued. We shall look at five New Testament passages that led them to that conclusion. To emphasize that nothing in this section is original, I shall frequently include quotations from leading writers.

## 1. Hebrews 1:1-2

> *God, who at various times and in various ways spoke in time past to the fathers by the prophets, has in these last days spoken to us by his Son...*

Here we have a contrast between revelation in the days of the old covenant and that given 'to us' in the new. The contrast should not be pressed too far — in both covenants it was *God* who spoke to his people. Nevertheless his manner of speaking under the two covenants was quite different. In the days of the former covenant God spoke 'at various times and in various ways' — in visions, dreams and 'face to face' — throughout the centuries of Israel's history, by many different people (the prophets). These revelations were partial and incomplete. In contrast to this, the new-covenant revelation comes *once*, in one person. And it is complete, since that one person is God's Son, who is 'the brightness of his glory and the express image of his person' (Heb. 1:3). The Puritan commentator Matthew Henry brings out the implications of this text:

> *The times of the gospel are the last times, the gospel revelation is the last we are to expect from God... [Now] we must expect no new revelation, but only more of the Spirit of Christ to help us better to understand what is already received... It is the final, the finishing revelation, given forth in the last days of divine revelation, to which nothing is to be added ... so that now the minds of men are no longer kept in suspense by the expectation of new discoveries, but they rejoice in a complete revelation of the will of God.*[10]

Another leading Puritan, John Owen, devoted eighty-four pages of his huge commentary on Hebrews to just the first two verses of the letter! But his conclusion is the same:

> *In opposition to this gradual revelation of the mind of God under the Old Testament, the apostle intimates that now by Jesus, the Messiah, the Lord hath at once begun and finished the whole revelation of his will ... no new revelation is to be expected, to the end of the world.*[11]

In his *Explanatory Notes upon the New Testament,* John Wesley, the great revival leader of the eighteenth century, understands this passage to prove 'the one entire and perfect revelation which [God] has made to us by Jesus Christ', and that therefore 'no other revelation is to be expected'.[12]

## 2. Jude 3

*Contend earnestly for the faith which was once for all delivered to the saints.*

It is generally accepted that by 'the faith' Jude means 'the body of Christian teaching', rather than the believer's trust in Christ. This was delivered 'once for all'. The significance of this is brought out by J. N. D. Kelly, writing in 1969: 'Christianity is viewed as a system of revealed teaching which is by its very nature unalterable and normative (this is the force of *once for all.*'[13]

This text thus rules out completely any ongoing view of revelation. The body of Christian teaching has been given once for all; it is unalterable; nothing must be added to it. The Puritan Thomas Manton, in expounding this verse, writes:

*Once for all, as never to be altered and changed; and when the canon or rule of faith was closed up, there was nothing to be added further, as a part of the authentic and infallible rule, though the daily necessities of the church do call for a further explication... Observe, that the doctrine of salvation was but once delivered, to remain for ever without variation... Well then, expect not new revelations or discoveries of new truths beside the word, which is the immutable rule of salvation.*[14]

## 3. Ephesians 2:20

*... having been built on the foundation of the apostles and prophets, Jesus Christ himself being the chief cornerstone...*

There are two technical questions that complicate the detailed interpretation of this passage:

1. By 'apostles and prophets', does Paul mean two distinct groups ('the apostles and the prophets'), or one group ('the apostles who are prophets')? Either interpretation is grammatically possible here.
2. If he does mean two distinct groups, by 'prophets' does he mean New Testament prophets, or those of the Old Testament?

There is not space here to discuss these matters adequately. However, the main thrust of the text is clear. The 'apostles and prophets' (whatever interpretation of the expression we adopt) were the agents of God's revelation to his people. Therefore the metaphor of 'the foundation' is hugely significant. The whole point about a foundation is that it is laid once and for all, at the beginning, and cannot be added to at some later time when the building is well under way. In fact Paul extends this architectural metaphor a little further: not only are the 'apostles and prophets' the foundation, but 'Jesus Christ himself' is 'the chief cornerstone' of the building. The inescapable implication of this is that the revelatory work of the 'apostles and prophets', like the work of Christ, is unique and unrepeatable. The conclusion is inevitable: no more revelation is to be expected and hence, of course, no more agents of revelation are to be expected.

A great preacher of the last century, Dr Martyn Lloyd-Jones, applied this text along the same lines:

> *There can be no repetition of apostles and prophets. They are the foundation. You do not repeat a foundation. A foundation is laid once and for ever... Obviously there can be no addition to this foundation. In the matter of teaching, I mean. If the foundation is the teaching of the apostles [and Lloyd-Jones believes that it is] you cannot add to it... You cannot add to a foundation, you cannot take from a foundation. Here is a corpus of truth, here is a body of doctrine. You cannot add, you cannot subtract, you cannot touch a foundation.*[15]

## 4. 2 Timothy 3:16-17

> *All Scripture is given by inspiration of God, and is profitable for doctrine, for reproof, for correction, for instruction in righteousness, that the man of God may be complete, thoroughly equipped for every good work.*

'Scripture' here should not be limited to the Old Testament. In 1 Timothy Paul quotes from Luke's Gospel and designates it as Scripture (see 1 Tim. 5:18). By the time that Paul is writing 2 Timothy it is very probable that most of the New Testament has been written. The point here, then, is that the will of God revealed in Scripture is sufficient to make Christians complete, fully equipped to serve their Lord. The great Reformer John Calvin gives the application of this:

> *Here complete means perfect, a man in whom there is nothing at all defective, for he asserts without qualification that the Scripture is sufficient to achieve perfection. Thus any man who is*

*not satisfied with the Scripture seeks to know more than he ought, and more than it is good for him to know.*[16]

The relevance of this to the question of prophecy today is obvious: no further revelation is needed; we should be satisfied with the Scripture.

At this point it is reasonable to pause and ask the question: 'What would an evangelical Charismatic make of this verse?' Wayne Grudem (who believes in prophecy today) discusses it in some detail in his *Systematic Theology*. He uses it to prove the doctrine of the sufficiency of Scripture, which he defines as follows:

> *The sufficiency of Scripture means that Scripture contained all the words of God he intended his people to have at each stage of redemptive history, and that it now contains all the words of God we need for salvation, for trusting him perfectly, and for obeying him perfectly.*[17]

This is a good definition. What role, then, can further revelation through a prophet play? Grudem explains further: 'The sufficiency of Scripture shows us that *no modern revelations from God are to be placed on a level equal to Scripture in authority.*'[18] Several questions immediately spring to mind here:

1. If Scripture is sufficient, it is reasonable for us to ask what need there is for modern revelations from God at all.

2. No evangelical Charismatic would ever want to go so far as to add a prophecy or revelation to the Bible

as an 'appendix', but if God were to give a revelation through a prophet in a church today would God not expect his people to respond to it? If it were a prediction, would God not expect that the recipients would believe it? If it were a command, would God not expect that those to whom it was given would obey it? The prophecy would therefore be for that congregation an addition to the Word of God — an extra belief or duty for them to believe or fulfil. For that congregation Scripture would have proved insufficient; God would be requiring something more from them — unless, that is, the prediction or command was one that was already found in the Bible; and in that case we might well ask, what would be the point of its being revealed again?

3. Does this therefore mean that Charismatic prophets cannot give any predictions or commands, except repeating those of the Bible? This seems to be the implication of Grudem's words:

> We must insist that God does not require us to believe anything about himself or his work in the world that is contained in these revelations but not in Scripture. And we must insist that God does not require us to obey any moral directives that come to us through such means but that are not confirmed by Scripture.[19]

If that is the case, then surely much of the attraction of having modern-day prophets is lost.

These problems were not apparent among the first Christian churches. When God, speaking through Agabus, predicted a famine, the hearers were duty-bound to believe it even though it could not be confirmed from Scripture. When revelation was given to the church at Antioch that Paul and Barnabas should be sent out as missionaries, the congregation was bound to obey, even though such specific guidance could not be confirmed by Scripture. This again illustrates the huge difference between the prophets of the New Testament churches and Charismatic prophets today.

This text (2 Tim. 3:16-17) therefore poses major problems for those who believe in continuing revelation. As Calvin wrote (in the passage quoted earlier), it teaches us that 'Any man who is not satisfied with the Scripture seeks to know more than he ought.'

## 5. Revelation 22:18-19

> For I testify to everyone who hears the words of the prophecy of this book: If anyone adds to these things, God will add to him the plagues that are written in this book; and if anyone takes away from the words of the book of this prophecy, God shall take away his part from the Book of Life, from the holy city, and from the things which are written in this book.

Undoubtedly these words refer primarily to the book of Revelation itself. However, occurring as they do in the last chapter of a book written by the last surviving apostle, they can be seen as applying to the whole of Scripture. Nothing is to be deleted from its contents, and no more revelation is to be added to it. This would explain the unparalleled severity of the warnings. The Puritan commentator Matthew Henry is therefore on firm ground in his comment:

*This sanction is like a flaming sword, to guard the canon of the Scripture from profane hands. Such a fence as this God set about the law (Deut. 4:2), and the whole Old Testament (Mal. 4:4), and now in the most solemn manner about the whole Bible, assuring us that it is a book of the most sacred nature, divine authority, and of the last importance, and therefore the peculiar care of the great God.* [20]

R. L. Thomas, in his commentary on Revelation (published in 1995) writes in similar vein:

*So the warnings about adding and taking away must pertain to teachers in the churches. They must be a prophetic protest against the spurious revelations that circulated through false teachers and false prophets in the name of the apostles. The commands here terminate any further prophecies that might arise through other prophets or prophetesses such as Jezebel (2:20)... The relation of the warning of vv. 18-19 to the 'canonization – formula' of Deut. 4:1 ff. is another good reason for concluding that John is forbidding any further use of the gift of prophecy. This is a canonizing of the book of Revelation parallel to the way the Deuteronomy passage came to apply to the whole OT canon. Use of the canonical model is equivalent to saying that there was no more room for inspired messages... So the final book of the Bible is also the concluding product of NT prophecy.* [21]

It is therefore natural to conclude from these verses that God has said all that he has to say to his people. Nothing more is to be added. Revelations from God, and the gift of prophecy that mediates them, are no longer to be given.

## The testimony of evangelicals through the centuries

It was scriptural arguments such as these that persuaded evangelicals from the Reformation onwards that the gift of prophecy was not intended by God to continue in the church. To make it clear that this is what the vast majority of evangelicals believed, we shall now permit them to express their belief in their own words. This is of particular importance because some of those quoted below have been said to have had Charismatic beliefs regarding prophecy.

### The Thirty-Nine Articles (sixteenth century)

These were the fundamental articles of faith of the Church of England reborn in the sixteenth-century Reformation. Therefore they represent the views of Cranmer and the other leading English Reformers.

> On the sufficiency of Holy Scripture for Salvation: Holy Scripture containeth all things necessary to salvation: so that whatsoever is not read therein, nor may be proved thereby, is not to be required of any man ... (Article VI).[22]

### Martin Luther (sixteenth century)

In his commentary on John 16:13 Luther writes:

> Now that the apostles have preached the Word and have given their writings, and nothing more than what they have written remains to be revealed, no new and special revelation or miracle is necessary... One does not need any new signs or miracles, since it

*was confirmed in the beginning ... miracles are no longer neces-*
*sary. Now no further words of revelation are to be expected.*[23]

## John Calvin (sixteenth century)

*Let this be a sure axiom — that there is no word of God to*
*which place should be given in the Church save that which is*
*contained, first, in the law and the Prophets; and, secondly, in the*
*writings of the apostles, and that the only due method of teaching*
*in the Church is according to the prescription and rule of this*
*word.*[24]

*The gift of tongues, and other such things, are ceased long ago*
*in the Church.*[25]

In fact Calvin did believe that the prophets mentioned in
Paul's letters had a continuing role to play in the life of the
church — but that is because he did not believe that they
were agents of revelation. Rather, according to Calvin:

*[Paul] means by prophets, not those endowed with the gift of*
*foretelling, but those who are blessed with the unique gift of deal-*
*ing with Scripture, not only by interpreting it, but also by the*
*wisdom they showed in making it meet the needs of the hour.*[26]

They were in fact, he believed, preachers who were specially
gifted in explaining and applying Scripture.

## The *Westminster Confession* (seventeenth century)

This was the doctrinal standard of the Presbyterian Church.
As these paragraphs are fully reproduced in *The Philadelphia*

*Confession of Faith* (of the American Baptists), in *The Baptist Confession of Faith of 1689* (English and Welsh Baptists) and in *The Savoy Declaration of Faith and Order* (1658, Congregationalists), they represented the views of the whole reformed church outside of the Church of England:

> *It pleased the Lord, at sundry times and in divers manners, to reveal himself, and to declare that his will unto his church; and afterwards ... to commit the same wholly unto writing; which maketh the holy scriptures to be most necessary; those former ways of God revealing his will unto his people being now ceased (1:1).*

> *The whole counsel of God, concerning all things necessary for his own glory, man's salvation, faith, and life, is either expressly set down in scripture, or by good and necessary consequence may be deduced from scripture: unto which nothing at any time is to be added, whether by new revelations of the Spirit, or traditions of men (1:VI).*

## Thomas Watson (Puritan, seventeenth century)

> *The Scripture is a full and perfect canon [i.e., rule of faith], containing in it all things necessary to salvation... It gives us an exact model of religion, and perfectly instructs us in the deep things of God.* [27]

> *In Christ's time and in the time of the apostles, there [were] then extraordinary gifts in the church which are now ceased.*[28]

### John Owen (Puritan, seventeenth century)

We have already quoted John Owen with reference to
Hebrews 1:1-2 to show that he believes that 'No new revelation is to be expected, to the end of the world.' In his *Works*
he writes:

> Gifts which in their own nature exceed the whole power of all
> our faculties, that dispensation of the Spirit is long since ceased
> and where it is now pretended unto by any, it may justly be sus-
> pected as an enthusiastic delusion.[29]

### Matthew Henry (Puritan, seventeenth to eighteenth centuries)

In the introduction to the fourth volume of his commentary
he states:

> The gift of tongues was one new product of the spirit of proph-
> ecy and given for a particular reason... These and other gifts of
> prophecy, being a sign, have long since ceased and been laid aside,
> and we have no encouragement to expect the revival of them; but,
> on the contrary, are directed to call the Scriptures the *more sure
> word of prophecy*, more sure than voices from heaven; and to them
> we are directed to *take heed*, to search them, and to hold them
> fast.[30]

### John Wesley (leader in the Methodist revival of the eigtheenth century)

He makes the following statement:

> ... the word of God, the writings of the Old and New Testa-
> ment ... is a lantern unto a Christian's feet, and a light in all his

*paths. This alone he receives as his rule of right or wrong, of whatever is really good or evil. He esteems nothing good, but what is here enjoined, either directly or by plain consequence; he accounts nothing evil but what is here forbidden, either in terms, or by undeniable inference. Whatever the Scripture neither forbids nor enjoins, either directly or by plain consequence, he believes to be of an indifferent nature; to be in itself neither good nor evil; this being the whole and sole outward rule whereby his conscience is to be directed in all things.*[31]

Commenting on Hebrews 1:1-2, he concludes that 'No other revelation is to be expected.[32]

Elsewhere he states:

*I deny that either I, or any in connection with me … do now, or ever did, lay claim to … extraordinary operations of the Spirit.*[33]

## George Whitefield (leader in the Methodist revival of the eighteenth century)

Writing to the Bishop of London, he says:

*The karismata, the miraculous gifts conferred on the primitive church … have long since ceased.*[34]

## Jonathan Edwards (leader in the Great Awakening, the revival in America in the eighteenth century)

In *Charity and its Fruits,* a detailed exposition of 1 Corinthians 13, he writes:

> The extraordinary gifts of the Spirit, such as the gift of tongues, of miracles, of prophecy, etc. ... are not given in the ordinary course of God's providence ... as they were bestowed on the prophets and apostles to enable them to reveal the mind and will of God before the canon of Scripture was complete... But since the canon of Scripture has been completed, and the Christian church fully founded and established, these extraordinary gifts have ceased.[35]

## Samuel Jarvis (eighteenth-century hymn-writer):

> How firm a foundation, ye saints of the Lord,
> Is laid for your faith in his excellent word!
> What more can he say than to you he hath said,
> You who unto Jesus for refuge have fled?[36]

## C. H. Spurgeon (famous Baptist preacher of the nineteenth century)

> Those works of the Holy Spirit which are at this time vouchsafed to the Church of God are every way as valuable as those earlier miraculous gifts which have departed from us. The work of the Holy Spirit, by which men are quickened from their death in sin, is not inferior to the power which made men speak with tongues.[37]

## Charles Hodge (American theologian of the nineteenth century)

> The Bible contains all the extant revelations of God ... so that nothing can rightfully be imposed on the consciences of men as truth or duty which is not directly or by necessary implication in the Holy Scriptures. [38]

*The fact that an office existed in the apostolic church is no evidence that it was intended to be permanent. In that age there was a plenitude of spiritual manifestations and endowments demanded for the organization and propagation of the church, which is no longer required. We have no longer prophets, nor workers of miracles, nor gifts of tongues.*[39]

## John Murray (twentieth-century theologian)

*Since we no longer have prophets, since we do not have our Lord with us as he was with his disciples, and since we do not have new organs of revelation as in apostolic times, Scripture in its total extent, according to the conception entertained by our Lord and his apostles, is the only revelation of the mind and will of God available to us. This is what the finality of Scripture means for us; it is the only extant revelatory Word of God.*[40]

## Dr Martyn Lloyd-Jones (twentieth-century preacher)

*There is to be no fresh revelation. There is no need of any. It was given and finally given to the apostles (see Jude 3).*[41]

# Scriptural arguments for the continuation of prophecy examined

Several arguments from Scripture are commonly referred to by Charismatics as evidence that the gift of prophecy was to continue in the church until the return of Christ, and we shall consider some of these now.

1. 'Scripture does not distinguish between temporary and lasting gifts'

It is commonly objected that it is entirely arbitrary for non-Charismatics to argue that some of the spiritual gifts have passed away but others have not, and that Scripture makes no distinction between 'ordinary' gifts that are permanent and 'extraordinary' gifts that were temporary.

*Response*

It is true that this distinction is not made in a formal way, but those who hold to it believe that it is forced on them by Scripture. For example, no evangelical believes that there are apostles in the church today with the authority of Peter and Paul. These men had unique qualifications — they had learned the gospel directly from Jesus; he had directly appointed them, and they were witnesses to his resurrection. This spiritual gift, the first in Paul's list in 1 Corinthians 12:28-29 ('first apostles …'), was therefore temporary. With regard to the gift of prophecy, it has been argued in the previous sections that its connection with revelation means that it too was not intended by God to continue beyond the New Testament period of revelation. Hence Paul uses the illustration of 'the foundation of the apostles and prophets' (Eph. 2:20), a metaphor that implies the cessation of both these gifts. So although in the sections of Scripture that list the gifts they are not distinguished in this way, nevertheless the distinction is scriptural.

2. The argument from Acts 2:16-21 (quoting the prophecy of Joel)

Here we read:

*But this is what was spoken by the prophet Joel:*

*'And it shall come to pass in the last days, says God,*
*That I will pour out of my Spirit on all flesh;*
*Your sons and your daughters shall prophesy,*
*Your young men shall see visions,*
*Your old men shall dream dreams.*
*And on my menservants and on my maidservants*
*I will pour out my Spirit in those days;*
*And they shall prophesy.*
*I will show wonders in heaven above*
*And signs in the earth beneath:*
*Blood and fire and vapour of smoke.*
*The sun shall be turned into darkness,*
*And the moon into blood,*
*Before the coming of the great and awesome day of the LORD.*
*And it shall come to pass*
*That whoever calls on the name of the LORD*
*Shall be saved.'*

It is argued that, since the phrase, 'the last days', refers to the period between Christ's first and second coming, then the gift of prophecy must continue until Christ's return.

*Response*

I would agree that this prophecy is a description of the entire church age and is not to be restricted to the initial outpouring of the Spirit. In this prophecy four things are promised, and each of them must equally be taken as being abiding characteristics of the age of the Spirit. They are:

1. The Spirit is poured out upon *all* types of people, regardless of race, age, sex, or social status.

2. The result of this happening is that they will *all* prophesy (seeing visions and dreaming dreams are of course intimately related to prophecy; see Num. 12:6).

3. Mighty signs in the sky and on the earth will be given.

4. *All* who call on the name of the Lord will be saved.

I believe that the second characteristic (that all the people of God will prophesy) should be understood in a figurative sense. In support of this I shall set out four reasons, which, when viewed together, leave no doubt in my mind that this is the correct interpretation:

In the first place, it is quite clear that many Old Testament prophecies are to be understood figuratively rather than in a strictly literal sense. Examples of this are:

- *Isaiah 40:3-5.* Mountains and valleys were not literally levelled during the ministry of John the Baptist!
- *Isaiah 66:21.* God would not literally take priests and Levites from among the Gentiles, but we understand it figuratively, as saying that the Gentiles too would have access into his presence to worship him.
- *Malachi 1:11.* Although the Gentiles would not literally offer up incense and other ceremonial offerings, they would indeed be brought to truly worship God — in other words, a figurative fulfilment.

For a few other examples selected from many, see Genesis 3:15; Isaiah 9:1-2; Jeremiah 30:9; Ezekiel 37:24-25; Malachi 4:5.

We should remember that the prophets spoke in language that was both vivid and meaningful for the people of their own day.

Secondly, it is clear that at least part of this prophecy of Joel is also to be understood figuratively. The promise of the great wonders and heavenly portents, including the sun being turned into darkness and the moon into blood, has never taken place in a literal sense. Since this promise too, however, is one of the abiding characteristics of the age of the Spirit, it must therefore be interpreted in a figurative sense.

Thirdly, a figurative interpretation of the reference to all the people prophesying makes sense. In the Old Testament it was especially the prophets who directly experienced God and the working of his Spirit (see, for example, Num. 11:17,25,29; 1 Sam. 10:6). In the new covenant, according to this prophecy, *all* the people of God would enjoy what under the old covenant was reserved for a few. Jeremiah gave the same message in different words: 'They shall all know me, from the least of them to the greatest of them' (Jer. 31:33-34).

Finally, if the promise is understood in a strictly literal sense to mean that all believers will prophesy, then it has simply not been fulfilled. It was not fulfilled even in the apostolic church, since Paul can ask, 'All are not prophets, are they?' (1 Cor. 12:29, NASB) — still less so in the centuries since then. Yet Joel's prophecy is an unconditional one to the people of God: 'I *will* in those days pour forth of my Spirit and they *shall* prophesy' (Acts 2:18, NASB, emphasis added). The great emphasis of the prophecy is that *every* believer will be indwelt by the Spirit and, if it is to be taken in a literal sense, that *every* believer will prophesy. The incontrovertible fact that not every believer prophesies shows that the promise is not meant to be interpreted literally.

These considerations lead me to conclude that this passage from Joel does not prove that the gift of prophecy was to remain until Christ's return.

### 3. 'This would make I Corinthians 14 and similar passages irrelevant to believers today'

It is commonly argued that passages like 1 Corinthians 14, with its detailed discussion of prophecy, would be rendered pointless if the gift has now passed away. Can a New Testament command such as 'Desire earnestly to prophesy' (1 Cor. 14:39) be ignored? Is this chapter now of historical interest only?

*Response*

To begin to answer this argument we can draw a parallel with the book of Leviticus. Although much of the direct relevance of that book passed away when the ceremonial law was abrogated, the principles which it teaches concerning the worship of God, the nature of the atonement, the types of Christ, and so on, are all still of immense value to the Christian today. Similarly, if the gift of prophecy has been withdrawn it does not mean that 1 Corinthians 14 only has value as a historical document. There are several principles in the chapter that are fundamental to the life and worship of today's churches. To give some examples:

- Love is to be our first aim, but spiritual gifts (those that continue) are also to be desired (v. 1).
- The aim of spiritual gifts is to edify the church (vv. 4,5,12).

- The worship of God is to be conducted in an orderly manner (vv. 26-33).
- All things must be done in submission to apostolic authority (v. 37).
- In the words of Matthew Henry, 'What cannot be understood can never edify'[42] — this is clearly the chief lesson of the chapter (see vv. 2-19).

But can a New Testament command be ignored? Usually not, of course — but there are just a few examples of commands that for particular reasons do not now apply directly to us. They are like the commands concerning sacrifices in Leviticus that we read, learn from, but do not literally obey. Jesus, for example, instructed the twelve not to 'go into the way of the Gentiles' (Matt. 10:5), but we do not therefore conclude that the gospel is not to be preached to the Gentiles today! Similarly, most evangelical Christians would not argue that because the Council of Jerusalem forbade the eating of food offered to idols (Acts 15:29), therefore we are still required to abstain from it today. The point of the command was to prevent Gentile Christians causing unnecessary offence to their Jewish brethren, and in fact Paul himself later permitted it with the proviso that it should cause no offence to others (1 Cor. 10:25-29). It should be noted that with both these two examples there is nothing in the immediate context of these commands to make it clear that they are temporary. We recognize that they no longer directly apply only because of the more complete teaching given in the rest of Scripture. In the same way, with the command to 'desire earnestly to prophesy', if the gift has been withdrawn because revelation is now complete then, I would argue, the command no longer applies in its literal sense.

### 4. 'I Corinthians 13 teaches that prophecy will continue until the return of Christ'

It is argued by some that in 1 Corinthians 13:8-13 Paul tells us that the gift of prophecy will continue until the return of Christ. There we read:

> *Love never fails. But whether there are prophecies, they will fail; whether there are tongues, they will cease; whether there is knowledge, it will vanish away. For we know in part and we prophesy in part. But when that which is perfect has come, then that which is in part will be done away. When I was a child, I spoke as a child, I understood as a child, I thought as a child; but when I became a man, I put away childish things. For now we see in a mirror, dimly, but then face to face. Now I know in part, but then I shall know just as I also am known. And now abide faith, hope, love, these three; but the greatest of these is love.*

*Response*

This is a complex passage and it is not possible in the limited space available here to give a detailed treatment of every aspect of it. Nevertheless the following points can be made.[43]

Firstly, the purpose of this section, like the rest of the chapter, is to show that love is the 'more excellent way', greater than the spiritual gifts. Here we see that the spiritual gifts are temporary, in contrast with love, which 'never fails'.

Secondly, it could hardly be by chance that the three spiritual gifts that Paul contrasts with love here are all gifts of revelation — prophecy, tongues and the word of knowledge.

Nor does he say, 'prophecy, tongues, knowledge, and the like'. It is specifically revelatory gifts that he describes as temporary and partial.

Thirdly, to help us to understand the passing away of two of these gifts (the word of knowledge and prophecy) Paul gives four parallel descriptions of how and why it will happen. Each description is a contrast between *now* (when Paul was writing the letter) and *then* (after prophecy and knowledge have passed away). For clarity we shall set them out in a table.

| Now | Then |
|---|---|
| *First description* (vv. 9-10) | |
| For we know in part, and we prophesy in part. | But when that which is perfect has come, then that which is in part will be done away. |
| *Second description* (v. 11) | |
| When I was a child, I spoke as a child, I understood as a child, I thought as a child … | … but when I became a man, I put away childish things. |
| *Third description* (v. 12) | |
| For now we see in a mirror dimly … | … but then face to face. |
| *Fourth description* (v. 12) | |
| Now I know in part… | … but then I shall know just as I also am known. |

We shall comment on these descriptions in due course.

Fourthly, in verse 13 the contrast between the permanence of love and the impermanence of the three revelatory gifts is concluded: 'And now abide faith, hope, love, these three; but the greatest of these is love.' It will be noticed that faith and hope have now been introduced alongside love; 'these three' abide, Paul tells us, in contrast to the three revelatory gifts.

Having introduced the passage, we can now begin to answer the question: 'Will the three revelatory gifts continue until the coming of the heavenly state?' In verse 8 we are told that prophecies, tongues and knowledge will pass away, and in verse 13 we are told that, in contrast, 'Now abide faith, hope, love, these three.' If the temporary gifts continue until the coming of heaven, then it follows that faith, hope and love (which, in contrast, abide) must remain with us in heaven itself. If, however, any of the three that 'abide' do not continue in heaven, but cease when it arrives, then we must deduce that the three that are temporary pass away *before* the coming of heaven, at some point during the church age. The crux of the issue is therefore this: do faith and hope continue into heaven? In fact we must be more specific: do faith and hope, *as Paul understands them,* continue into heaven? It is not sufficient for us to suggest aspects of faith and hope that may continue into heaven — it is what Paul meant by these terms that counts.

I am confident that if anyone takes the trouble to look at all the references to 'hope' in Paul's writings they will discover two things. Firstly, there is no evidence that the thought of a hope possessed in heaven ever crossed Paul's mind (or indeed that of any other New Testament writer). Secondly, on the vast majority of occasions (if not on every occasion) when Paul speaks of the hope of Christians in general, he is speaking of their hope of heaven. This is particularly evident in Romans 8:23-25, which is surely the fullest passage in Paul's writings on the subject of hope. We shall quote the passage in full:

> *Not only that, but we also who have the firstfruits of the Spirit, even we ourselves groan within ourselves, eagerly waiting for the adoption, the redemption of our body. For we were saved in this hope, but hope that is seen is not hope; for why does one still hope for what he sees? But if we hope for what we do not see, then we eagerly wait for it with perseverance.*

In these three verses the word 'hope' is used five times and 'eagerly wait[ing]' occurs twice. And what is it that Christians hope and eagerly wait for? They are 'eagerly waiting *for the adoption, the redemption of our body'* — that is, the resurrection and the heavenly state. The idea of hope as expectation in heaven is nowhere in sight. For Paul and the first Christians their hope was of the glory to come. It was this militant, strength-giving hope — a quality that would garrison their hearts and enable them to endure in the fiercest of trials — that Paul wanted them to value along with faith and love as being far better than tongues, prophecy and knowledge. This hope would abide until the coming of heaven, at which point it would be fulfilled. The same argument could be made about faith. Paul wrote to the Corinthian church that 'We walk by faith, not by sight' (2 Cor. 5:7).

The conclusion, then, is hard to avoid: since two of the three that 'abide' are fulfilled when heaven comes, the three that are temporary must pass away before then. This passage tells us that prophecy, tongues and knowledge will pass away *before the coming of heaven.*

We must now turn our attention to the other verses that
describe the passing of prophecy and the gift of the word of
knowledge (1 Cor. 13:9-12). They pass away 'when that
which is perfect [or 'complete', as it could be translated] has
come'. This cannot be a reference to Christ as the words are
in the neuter, not the masculine form (i.e. it is a perfect thing,
not a perfect man). The other most common interpretations
are that it means either the eternal heavenly state, or the
completed revelation that became our New Testament.
Although neither of these is described anywhere else in the
Bible as 'that which is perfect', both would make reasonable
sense as far as this phrase is concerned. However, there are
considerable difficulties with the first interpretation, as has
already been shown. What we now need to see is whether
the second interpretation fits in with the four parallel descriptions of verses 9-12.

*First description* (vv. 9-10)
It makes perfect sense that partial methods of revelation
should be made redundant by the coming of a complete
revelation.

*Second description* (v. 11)
The image of a child putting away childish things when he
becomes a man again makes perfect sense. The passing of the
partial gifts is natural when the complete revelation comes,
and should not be lamented.

*Third description* (v. 12)
Although the expression 'face to face' immediately makes us
think of heaven, this in fact should not be the case. The
phrase may simply be a way of saying that we shall 'see

clearly' — after all, we do not literally 'see in a mirror, dimly' now. So the meaning may simply be: 'Now we see dimly, but then we shall see clearly.' However, the expression has an Old Testament background that is very illuminating. Seeing God 'face to face' is mentioned on eight other occasions in the Bible (if we include the obviously parallel expressions 'mouth to mouth' and 'eye to eye'), all of them in the Old Testament. It is interesting that only two of these passages refer to a literal face-to-face sight of God (Gen. 32:30; Judg. 6:22). The other references all refer to the experience of Israel in the wilderness (Num. 14:14; Deut. 5:24; Ezek. 20:35-36) or, particularly, to the experience of Moses (Exod. 33:11; Num. 12:8; Deut. 34:10). None of these refers to a literal vision of the face of God because we are told that Israel 'saw no form when the LORD spoke' to them (Deut. 4:15), and that even when Moses was given a vision of the glory of God, he did not see God's face (Exod. 33:23).

In what sense, then, did Moses see God 'face to face'? Numbers 12:6-8 is a key passage. God says here:

> *If there is a prophet among you,*
> *I, the LORD, make myself known to him in a vision;*
> *I speak to him in a dream.*
> *Not so with my servant Moses;*
> *He is faithful in all my house.*
> *I speak with him face to face,*
> *Even plainly, and not in dark sayings;*
> *And he sees the form of the LORD.*

In this passage we have a contrast between prophets who are given the word 'dimly' (in visions or dreams) and Moses, to whom God speaks 'plainly, and not in dark sayings'. Thus Moses experienced God face to face by receiving clear verbal revelation from him. It had nothing to do with heaven, but much to do with clear revelation. The similarities between this passage and 1 Corinthians 13:12 are such that it is very likely that Paul had this passage in mind. Therefore again we see that this description fits well with 'that which is perfect' being a full and clear verbal revelation from God received in this life.

*Fourth description* (v. 12)

This is probably the most difficult of the four descriptions, but this is equally the case whichever of the suggested interpretations one adopts. Whether on earth or in heaven, how can a finite creature know the infinite God just as much as he is known by God? God fully knows us, but how can we ever fully know him? It must mean that we know fully in a more limited sense, and could therefore refer to that completeness/perfection/maturity that the man of God can attain through the study of Scripture (2 Tim. 3:17), which, after all, contains 'the whole counsel of God' (Acts 20:27) and 'all truth' (John 16:13).

In conclusion, then, I believe that 1 Corinthians 13:8-13, far from proving the permanence of spiritual gifts, actually leads to the opposite conclusion. The three revelatory gifts mentioned pass away before the coming of the heavenly state, being made redundant by the coming of a complete verbal revelation. Of the three virtues that abide, faith and hope continue until heaven. Beyond that love alone contin-ues, because love alone 'never fails'. Hence 'The greatest of these is love.'

I readily acknowledge that many reformed and evangelical commentators would interpret 'that which is perfect' as a
reference to heaven. As examples we could mention John
Calvin, Matthew Henry and Charles Hodge. Yet despite this,
all these men for other reasons did not believe that prophecy
continued in the church (as we have seen). The difficulty of
this passage is well illustrated by Jonathan Edwards in his
discussion of it in his book, *Charity and its fruits*. Edwards
was a great theologian as well as preacher and revival leader,
yet he interprets the passage both ways![44] For most people,
therefore, it has been other, clearer passages that have
determined their conclusion on the subject of prophecy.

# CONCLUSION

# Conclusion

In summarizing the use of the word *prophētēs* ('prophet') in the Greek-speaking world before and at the time of Jesus, Krämer writes, 'It denotes the one who speaks in the name of a god, declaring the divine will and counsel in the oracle… He is the mouthpiece of the god.'[1] As we have seen, this is also its significance in the Bible. The difference between the pagan prophets of the Greek world and those of the Old and New Testaments consisted in this: the biblical prophets spoke in the name of the LORD, the living and true God, and therefore they were preserved from all error. Moses and Isaiah, Agabus and John all spoke with divine authority, as 'Thus says the LORD…' Certainly the revelations given to some were of far greater significance than those given to others. They fulfilled widely differing roles in the plan of God. Yet the same intrinsic authority was given to each when they prophesied: they spoke the very word of God.

That was the conclusion to which our enquiries in chapter 2 led. There are not two levels of true prophecy in Scripture. Prophecy with error is false prophecy, and false prophecy is the mark of the false prophet.

As we saw in chapter 3, this raises serious questions about the prophecy that is common among many Christian fellowships in these days. Great claims are made for this prophecy. Clifford Hill, for example, writes that prophecy 'is a direct

word from the Lord', 'the eyes and ears of the church', that it
is 'essential for … the carrying out of the Great Commission',
and that ignoring it brings 'disastrous consequences'.[2]
Donald Gee tells us that it is 'a supernatural feature' and a
'vital element' of New Testament ministry.[3] In making such
claims they are not untypical of Charismatics. Yet in that
chapter we also saw that by 'prophecy' these same people
were speaking of a phenomenon that could be completely in
error, and that commands and predictions especially should
be treated with great suspicion! By biblical standards this is
not prophecy at all. In particular it has little in common with
the actual examples of New Testament prophecy that we are
given.

This difference between prophecy then and prophecy
now led on to the question of whether Christians should be
expecting further revelation today. We saw briefly that
leading evangelical Christians of past centuries have believed that God had withdrawn the gift of prophecy and that
the completion of the apostolic record of the gospel of Christ
in the New Testament had brought God's process of revelation to his people to an end. This, we saw, was based on
their interpretation of the New Testament itself.

Moreover they did not regard this as having left the
church disadvantaged, as if we now had insufficient or no
direct divine word for our guidance. On the contrary, in the
words of Matthew Henry quoted earlier, 'Now the minds of
men are no longer kept in suspense by the expectation of
new discoveries, but they rejoice in a complete revelation of
the will of God.' It is a great blessing to the church that now,
in the words of Martin Luther, 'No new and special revelation … is necessary'! Nor should we ever lose sight of the
fact that this *written* Word of God 'is living and powerful,

and sharper than any two-edged sword' (Heb. 4:12). For the writer of Hebrews is not making this affirmation about some current gift of prophecy, but about *Scripture*, having just quoted from Psalm 95 — along, of course, with many other Old Testament passages in the rest of the letter.

The implications of all this are far-reaching. In particular, if the theses of this book are correct, then it calls for a radical reassessment of the claims of the Charismatic Movement. Though we can honour our Charismatic brothers and sisters for their zeal in evangelism and for their scriptural emphasis on every Christian having a ministry within the body of Christ, yet in this area of prophecy we must surely ask them to think again. Only in Scripture do we now have the true Word of God. This Word alone endures for ever and is a sure resting place for the faith and hope of the children of God.

# NOTES

# Notes

## Chapter 1 — The distinguishing characteristics of prophecy in Israel

1. *The Works of B. B. Warfield,* Baker, 1981, vol. 1, pp.82-3.
2. E. J. Young, *My Servants the Prophets,* Eerdmans, 1952, p.54.
3. D. E. Aune, *Prophecy in Early Christianity and the Ancient Mediterranean World,* Eerdmans, 1983, p.17.

## Chapter 2 — Prophecy in the New Testament church

1. Gerhard Friedrich, *Theological Dictionary of the New Testament,* ed. Gerhard Kittel, Eerdmans, 1968, vol. VI, p.828.
2. *Ibid.,* p.196.
3. Wayne A. Grudem, *The Gift of Prophecy in 1 Corinthians,* University Press of America, 1982, p.63.
4. Leon Morris, *The First and Second Epistles to the Thessalonians,* Eerdmans, 1959, p.177.
5. Grudem, *The Gift of Prophecy in 1 Corinthians,* p.63.
6. Wayne Grudem, *Systematic Theology,* Inter-Varsity Press, 1994, p.1054.
7. Grudem, *The Gift of Prophecy in 1 Corinthians,* pp.64-5.
8. H. M. F. Büchsel, *Theological Dictionary of the New Testament,* ed. Gerhard Kittel, Eerdmans, 1965, vol. III, p.947.
9. C. K. Barrett, *The First Epistle to the Corinthians,* Black, 1968, p.286.
10. R. C. H. Lenski, *The Interpretation of the Acts of the Apostles,* Augsburg Publishing House, 1961, p.869.
11. Grudem, *The Gift of Prophecy in 1 Corinthians,* p.79.
12. See chapter 5 of Patrick Fairbairn, *The Interpretation of Prophecy,* Banner of Truth, 1964, for a fuller treatment of this subject.

13. W. A. Grudem, *The Gift of Prophecy in the New Testament and Today*, Crossway Books, 1988, p.97.

14. F. F. Bruce, *The Acts of the Apostles*, Tyndale Press, 1951, p.385.

15. See, for example, the discussions of this passage in the commentaries on Acts by John Calvin; John Stott, *The Message of Acts*, Inter-Varsity Press, 1994; I. Howard Marshall, *Tyndale New Testament Commentaries*, Inter-Varsity Press, 1980.

**Chapter 3 — Prophecy now**

1. Donald Gee, *Concerning Spiritual Gifts*, The Gospel Publishing House, Missouri, 1928, pp.47-8.

2. Dennis and Rita Bennett, *The Holy Spirit and You*, Kingsway, 1971, pp. 115-17.

3. Donald Bridge and David Phypers, *Spiritual Gifts and the Church*, Inter-Varsity Press, 1973, p.41.

4. Clifford Hill, *Prophecy Past and Present*, Eagle, 1989, p.303.

5. Grudem, *Systematic Theology*, p.1055.

6. *Ibid.*, p.1059.

7. David Wilkerson, *The Vision*, Spire Books, 1974, pp.11, 54, 35.

8. This example is given by Eric E. Wright in *Strange Fire*, Evangelical Press, 1996, p.287.

9. See Wright, *Strange Fire*, p.287.

10. Matthew Henry, *Commentary on the Whole Bible*, Hendrickson, 1991, p.2380 (comments on Hebrews 1:1-3).

11. *The Works of John Owen, DD*, T. & T. Clark, 1862, vol. XX, pp.19-20.

12. John Wesley, *Explanatory Notes upon the New Testament*, The Epworth Press, 1950, p. 810.

13. J. N. D. Kelly, *The Epistles of Peter and of Jude*, A. and C. Black, 1969, p.248.

14. Thomas Manton, *Works*, vol. 5, London, 1871, p. 111.

15. D. Martyn Lloyd-Jones, *God's way of reconciliation: Ephesians two*, The Banner of Truth Trust, 1972, pp. 446-7.

16. John Calvin, *Calvin's Commentaries: The Second Epistle of Paul the Apostle to the Corinthians and the Epistles to Timothy, Titus and*

*Philemon*, Oliver and Boyd, Edinburgh, 1964, p.331 (comments on 2 Timothy 3:17).

17. Grudem, *Systematic Theology*, p.127.

18. *Ibid.*, pp.131-2, emphasis his.

19. *Ibid.*, p.132.

20. Henry, *Commentary*, p.2485 (comments on Revelation 22:18-19).

21. R. L. Thomas, *Revelation 8-22: An Exegetical Commentary*, Moody Press, 1995, pp.516-17.

22. The 'Articles of Religion' of the Church of England are found at the end of the *Book of Common Prayer*.

23. Martin Luther, *Luther's Works*, Concordia Publishing House, 1961, vol. 24, pp. 367-8.

24. John Calvin, *Institutes of the Christian Religion*, IV, viii, 8.

25. John Calvin, *Calvin's Commentaries: The Acts of the Apostles, 1-13*, Oliver and Boyd, Edinburgh, 1965, p.317 (comments on Acts 10:44).

26. John Calvin, *Calvin's Commentaries: The First Epistle of Paul the Apostle to the Corinthians*, Oliver and Boyd, Edinburgh, 1960, p.271 (comments on 1 Corinthians 12:28).

27. Thomas Watson, *A Body of Divinity*, The Banner of Truth Trust, 1958, p.21.

28. Thomas Watson, *The Beatitudes*, The Banner of Truth Trust, 1971, p.14.

29. *The Works of John Owen, DD*, T. & T. Clark, 1862, vol. IV, p.518.

30. Henry, *Commentary*, Original Preface to vol. IV, p. xvi.

31. John Wesley, *Forty-Four Sermons*, The Epworth Press, 1944, p.125 (Sermon XI, section 6).

32. John Wesley, *Explanatory Notes upon the New Testament*, The Epworth Press, 1950, p.810.

33. A letter dated 4 November 1758, in *The Letters of the Rev. John Wesley*, The Epworth Press, 1931.

34. George Whitefield, 'Second letter to the Bishop of London', *Works* (edited by John Gillies), Edward and Charles Dilly, London, 1771, vol. IV, p. 167.

35. Jonathan Edwards, *Charity and its Fruits*, The Banner of Truth Trust, 1969, p.29.

36. This hymn is found in many different evangelical hymn-books — e.g. *Christian Hymns*, Evangelical Movement of Wales, 1977, no. 574.

37. C. H. Spurgeon, *Metropolitan Tabernacle Pulpit*, The Banner of Truth Trust, vol. 30, page 386.

38. Charles Hodge, *Systematic Theology*, Thomas Nelson and sons, 1871, vol. I, p.183.

39. Charles Hodge, *1 & 2 Corinthians*, The Banner of Truth Trust, 1974, pp. 262-3 (comment on 1 Corinthians 12:28).

40. *The Collected Writings of John Murray*, The Banner of Truth Trust, 1976, vol. I, p.19.

41. D. Martyn Lloyd-Jones, *Authority*, Inter-Varsity Fellowship, 1958, p.59.

42. Henry, *Commentary*, p.2269 (comments on 1 Corinthians 14:1-5).

43. I am particularly indebted to an unpublished thesis by Stuart Olyott for much of the material for this section.

44. See especially Edwards' discussion of this passage on pp.324-5 of *Charity and its Fruits*, The Banner of Truth Trust, 1969. There he argues that 'There is a twofold *imperfect*, and so a twofold *perfect* state of the Christian Church', though he concludes that Paul has in mind 'especially ... the latter' (i.e. heaven).

## Conclusion

1. Helmut Krämer, *Theological Dictionary of the New Testament*, ed. Kittel, vol. VI, p.795.

2. Hill, *Prophecy Past and Present*, pp.214, 205, 226.

3. Gee, *Concerning Spiritual Gifts*, pp.2, 45.

A wide range of Christian books is available from Evangelical Press. If you would like a free catalogue please write to us or contact us by e-mail. Alternatively, you can view the whole catalogue online at our website: www.evangelicalpress.org.

Evangelical Press
Faverdale North, Darlington, Co. Durham, DL3 0PH, England

e-mail: sales@evangelicalpress.org

Evangelical Press USA
P. O. Box 825, Webster, New York 14580, USA

e-mail: usa.sales@evangelicalpress.org